SPECIAL OPS

America's Elite Forces in 21st Century Combat

Fred J. Pushies

MBI Publishing Company

This edition first published in 2003 by MBI Publishing Company, Galtier Plaza, Suite 200, 380 Jackson Street, St. Paul, MN 55101-3885 USA

MBI Publishing Company titles are also available at discounts in bulk quantity for industrial or sales-promotional use. For details write to Special Sales Manager at Motorbooks International Wholesalers & Distributors, Galtier Plaza, Suite 200, 380 Jackson Street, St. Paul, MN 55101-3885 USA

ISBN 0-7603-1603-1

Edited by Steve Gansen
Designed by Stephanie Michaud
Layout by Chris Fayers

Printed in USA

On the front cover: (left)"Green Berets" have special mobility teams who are experts in long-range, behind-the-line penetration. (right) U.S. Marines assigned to 2nd Battalion, 2nd Marines, Echo Company, 24th Marine Expeditionary Unit–Special Operations Capable (MEU(SOC)) disembark from an amphibious assault vehicle (AAV) to conduct a live-fire exercise.

On the frontispiece:
The advance combat optical gunsight (ACOG) is often used in daylight, filed operations. The ACOG's four-power sight gives the shooter an up-close-and-personal view of the enemy with a special reticle allowing him to range his target at various distances. An AFSOC PJ in HALO gear with M4 at the ready.

On the back cover: This trio of MH-60 Blackhawks from the 160th Special Operations Aviation Regiment (Airborne) includes a pair of MH-60 Blackhawks, with an MH-47 in the background. Their primary mission is the insertion, extraction, and resupply of U.S. SOF operators. Many consider the pilots of these helicopters to be the best in the world.

About the author: Fred Pushies has spent the last 15 years in the company of each of the units assigned to United States Special Operations Command (SOCOM). Fred has traveled extensively as a photographer and writer, from the mountains of the Rangers' training camp, to the desert with Special Forces mobility teams–the same teams that are now active in the Iraqi wasteland.

Fred has spent countless hours in Air Force Special Operations Command (AFSOC) Spectre gunships and Pave Low helicopters, as well as flying at treetop level with the 160th Special Operations Aviation Regiment. He has skimmed across the waves with the SEALs in a Mark V and crunched through the brush with Force Recon Marines. Fred's integrity and insight are evident in his previous works: *U.S. Air Force Special Ops, U.S. Army Special Forces,* and *Marine Force Recon.*

CONTENTS

Dedication

To those who stand on the wall . . .

Acknowledgments

I personally express my thanks to the Almighty God. May His gracious hand protect those who defend our freedom. My thanks to my wife Tammy and to my family for their continued support during my many trips, hours of interviews, and dinners missed. I thank the following individuals for their assistance in making this book possible: my editor, Steve Gansen, Motorbooks International, for the insight, support, and encouragement in this project; Bruce E. Zielsdorf, U.S. Army Public Affairs, New York; Carol Darby, USASOC Public Affairs, Fort Bragg, North Carolina; Chet Justice, U.S. SOCOM Public Affairs, MacDill Air Force Base, Florida; Public Affairs Offices of the Central Intelligence Agency; National Imagery and Mapping Agency; U.S. Central Command; Kathy Vinson, Defense Visual Information Center, March Air Reserve Base, California; Marc Stanley and Brent Westhoven, Advance Vehicle Systems, Inc.; and Oded Nechushtan, Flyer Defense, LLC.

INTRODUCTION

Corporal Ahmed Khamees stands his post in a residential area on the outskirts of Baghdad, in front of a house that by Western standards would be considered austere. But a house such as this, with its stone terrace and sturdy brickwork, is deemed luxurious here in the Iraqi capital.

The corporal glances at his watch, the old luminous hands barely visible under the glow of the crescent moon—2:00 a.m. . . .

Promising to declare its secret weapons programs to the United Nations, Iraq submitted its "official" 12,200-page report on December 7, 2002. Meanwhile, Saddam Hussein became concerned the United States would seek alternative measures to acquire confirmation of his country's claims through "unofficial" methods.

For this reason, Saddam ordered the Iraqi Internal Security Force to sequester the country's top scientists in the field of nuclear, biological and chemical weapons, scattering them around various compounds, buildings and houses, "for their own safety." The scientists' families were also under the watchful protection of security guards—again merely as a "precaution."

. . . Thus, here stands Corporal Khamees, counting the minutes on another long, boring night patrol. But before the portly guard can raise his head from checking his watch, a black-gloved hand covers his mouth. Another grasps the base of his head. In one swift action, snap!, his neck is broken. As the assailant slowly places the body of the lifeless guard in the bushes, he whispers into his communication gear, "North side—clear."

Affixed to his ear is a bone microphone that works by translating the vibrations in his skull into electronic voice signals, picking up the slightest sound and transmitting it at an audible signal. At the same time he hears in his headset, "South—clear."

A stack of four men approach the rear door to the house. They are dressed in Nomex assault suits with vests covering their torsos. On their heads are modular/integrated communications helmet (MICH) headgear with AN/PVS-14 night vision devices attached. Behind the nocturnal monocular they each sport a Nomex balaclava, which resembles a ski mask. The purpose of the balaclava is threefold. First, it protects the identity of the wearer; second, it protects him from flash-bang grenade explosions; and finally, it presents an image to enemy that the operator is "as serious as a "heart attack." Each of the men is armed with a Colt M4A1 carbine, fitted with a Knight Armament suppressor and AN/PEQ-2 IR laser targeting device.

Three of the men provide security while the fourth works on the lock on the wooden door. A telltale "click" of the lock tells him he has successfully gained entry. The door now open, the four-man team enters the building as one. Just as in their countless rehearsals, they maneuver from room to room, neutralizing one additional guard as they advance toward their objective: Dr. Hashmin Kassid. On the second floor, they reach the room in which the physicist is billeted. They rush in.

Dr. Kassid begins to rise from his bed. Two team members quickly restrict his movements, and the leader approaches the scientist. After running through a set of prearranged codes, he signals the other team members to relax their hold on the man. The team leader directs his next commentary into his headset, "Target Alpha Sierra. Precious cargo in hand. Ready for exfil."

The four-man assault team, with their objective in tow, heads down the stairs. Just as they reach the outer courtyard, they hear the rhythmic "whomp whomp whomp" of helicopter rotors approaching from the south. Within minutes, an MH-6 "Little Bird" lands in the front yard, the pilot homing in on the IR strobe held by one of the men in the security element.

For a moment the defecting man hesitates. He pulls at the shoulder of the team leader, "I was promised you would get my family out, too. I cannot go if they are not safe."

Without uttering a word the team leader grabs the scientist and ushers him to the awaiting helicopter. The man is confounded, and then he sees, sitting in the rear seat of the small aircraft, his wife and year-old son. Then, and only then, does the team leader talk to him: "Are you ready now, sir?"

"Yes, yes. Thank you, thank you."

The physicist takes a seat next to his wife, and they embrace.

Staff Sergeant Noel Hickman signals to the rest of the team, who board the MH-6. One man sits on each side of the "precious cargo" while the others sit on special benches affixed to the outside of the helicopter.

As the helicopter rises into the night and securely out of Baghdad, Dr. Hashmin Kassid reaches into his coat pocket. He hands Staff Sergeant Hickman three CDs. "I think your government will find this most interesting reading." The sergeant nods and places the CDs in the pocket of his assault vest, as the Little Bird disappears into the night. . . .

The above action depicts the extraction of an Iraqi nuclear physicist by a team of Delta Force operators and extracted by the "Night Stalkers." Although this is purely a hypothetical scenario, the United States Special Operations forces are fully capable of conducting such a mission.

CHAPTER ONE

BEHIND THE LINES

SPECIAL OPERATIONS COMMAND (SOCOM)

The United States Special Operations Command was established as a unified combatant command on April 16, 1987. A four-star general is in charge of this command, located at MacDill Air Force Base, Tampa, Florida. SOCOM has three service component commands: Naval Special Warfare Command, Fort Bragg, North Carolina; Naval Special Warfare Command, Coronado, California; Air Force Special Operations Command, Hurlburt Field, Florida; and Joint Special Operations Command, Pope Air Force Base, North Carolina.

The mission of SOCOM is to provide special operations forces to National Command Authority, regional combatant commanders, and American ambassadors and their country's teams during both peace and war. SOCOM prepares special operations forces to successfully conduct special operations, including civil affairs and psychological operations.

There are six special operations commands supporting geographic combatant commanders worldwide: Special Operations Command Atlantic, Special Operations Command Central, Special Operations Command Europe, Special Operations Command Pacific, Special Operations Command Korea, and Special Operations Command South.

When the media and others use the term "special forces," many people think of the various elite units of the U.S. military, including the Navy SEALs, the Army Rangers, and the Green Berets. In correct military parlance, the term refers exclusively to the U.S. Army Special Forces, traditionally known as the "Green Berets." The collection of the various U.S. Army, Navy, and Air Force commandos are defined as "special operations forces" and come under the command and control of SOCOM.

U.S. Special Operations forces are small units that work alone or in combination with one another in both direct and indirect military operations, often using tactics of unconventional warfare. These "quiet professionals" as they are often called, are trained in the newest methods, tactics, and procedures, and are equipped with the latest technology and weaponry. The soldiers, sailors, marines, and airmen who constitute SOCOM units exceed the capabilities of conventional military forces. Each of the services' units cross-train in many of the same

techniques, tactics, and procedures. There are times when their missions, frequently clandestine and often politically sensitive in nature, overlap. In military operations other than war (MOOTW), it may be necessary to deploy a small force to stealthily accomplish missions directed from National Command Authority. Such missions would be assigned to the appropriate SOF unit.

U.S. ARMY SPECIAL OPERATIONS COMMAND

Special Forces

U.S. Army Special Forces Command (Airborne) (USASFC(A)) commands seven major subordinate units. These units, known as special forces groups, are each commanded by a colonel. The mission statement of the special forces command is as follows: "To organize, equip, train, validate and prepare forces for deployment to conduct worldwide special

Here is a look inside the Tactical Operations Center (TOC) in Qatar, which has provided on-the-scene command and control for operations in Iraq. *Qatar Defense Visual Information Center*

operations, across the range of military operations, in support of regional combatant commanders, American ambassadors and other agencies as directed."

The 5th Special Forces Group (Airborne) is the primary SF group for CENTCOM's area of responsibility and has maintained a forward deployed battalion in Kuwait since Desert Storm. This battalion is outfitted with prepositioned equipment and vehicles, ready when called upon for immediate action. Operational Detachment–Alpha (ODA) will rotate through the region, thus keeping its knowledge of the area and interaction with the indigenous troops current. The Army's twelve-man, independent-minded ODAs, formerly known as A-teams, are at the heart of U.S. Special Forces operations.

In addition to their military skills, SF soldiers are also schooled in the culture, traditions, and language of the regions in which they operate. This ability makes them proficient in behind-the-lines, covert, and unconventional warfare missions.

Rangers

The 75th Ranger Regiment is the Army's premiere special operations

U.S. Army Special Forces, known as the "Green Berets" have special mobility teams who are experts in long-range, behind-the-line penetration. Additionally, the 5th Special Forces Group maintains a battalion in Kuwait. Such special forces assets enhance U.S. Special Operations Command Central's (SOCCENT's) power in the region. *Defense Visual Information Center*

light infantry rapid assault force. Their primary mission involves direct action-predominate operations. They have a singular purpose: to kill the enemy and break things. Their specialty is airfield seizure, though they are also more than capable of conducting raids, combat search and rescue (CSAR), and special equipment, and many other types of light infantry operations. They may be inserted and extracted by land, sea, or air. Ranger units focus on mission-essential tasks, including movement to contact, ambush, reconnoiter, perform airborne and air assaults, and perform hasty defense maneuvers.

The Ranger Regiment maintains a constant state of readiness, or Ready Reaction Force 1 (RRF). This means on any given day there is at least one Ranger battalion ready to deploy anywhere in the world within eighteen hours. Additionally, one rifle company with battalion command and control is ready to deploy in nine hours.

160th Special Operations Aviation Regiment (Airborne)

The 160th Special Operations Aviation Regiment (Airborne) provides aviation support to U.S. Special Operations forces. Primarily an Army asset, the 160th has a close working relationship with other units under SOCOM command. The majority of their missions occur under the cover of darkness; hence the unit nickname, the "Night Stalkers." The Regiment is comprised of modified OH-6 light observation helicopters, MH-60 Blackhawk utility helicopters, and MH-47 Chinook medium-lift helicopters. Additionally, the 160th have modified Little Bird and Blackhawk helicopters as AH-6 and MH-60 direct action penetrator (DAP) configured for close air support (CAS) missions. Their specialty is the covert insertion, re-supply and extraction of SOF teams. Additionally they may conduct armed escort, reconnaissance, surveillance, and electronic warfare in support of missions. The unit is the home of the "hottest" aviators in the Army, and some operators would extend that to ". . . in the world."

The Night Stalkers maintain several types of helicopters in their inventory, from the small and agile Little Bird, to the large size Chinook. Whether special operations forces need to perform a fast rope insertion/extraction (FRIES) on a roof top, request close air support, or extract from a "hot" landing zone, the 160th SOAR(A) has the aircraft, pilots and aircrews to accomplish the task. The unit's motto: "Night Stalkers Don't Quit!" These consummate flyers are the perfect complement to the covert SOF warriors.

AIR FORCE SPECIAL OPERATIONS COMMAND (AFSOC)

Air Force Special Operations Command is the air force element of the U.S. Special Operations Command. Its mission is to provide mobility, surgical firepower, covert tanker support, and special tactics teams. These units normally operate in concert with U.S. Army and Navy special operation forces, including special forces, Rangers, Special Operations Aviation Regiment, SEAL teams, psychological operations (PSYOP) forces, and civil affairs units. AFSOC supports a wide range of activities from combat operations of a limited duration to longer-term conflicts. They also provide support to foreign governments and their militaries. Dependent on shifting priorities, AFSOC maintains a flexible profile, allowing it to respond to numerous missions.

AFSOC brings the "big guns" in to support any SOF mission—From the AC-130U "Spectre" gunships bristling with 25mm chaingun, 40mm Bofors and 105mm howitzer cannon, to the correspondingly lethal MH-53 Pave Low helicopter.

The U.S. Army Rangers are Special Operations Command's (SOCOM's) premier light infantry assault force. Whether tasked with seizing an enemy airfield or providing the security element for a Delta Force raid, the members of the 75th Ranger Regiment are without equal in the world of light infantry. *USASOC*

Special Tactics Squadron

In addition to its awesome airpower, AFSOC may deploy special tactics squadrons comprised of combat control teams (CCTs) and pararescue jumpers (PJs). Special tactics teams (STTs) are proficient in sea-air-land insertion tactics into forward, non-permissive environments. The CCTs establish assault zones with air traffic control (ATC) capabilities. Assault zones could be a drop zone for a parachute deployment, a landing zone for heliborne operations, or for follow-on fixed-wing aircraft, for an extraction, or for low level re-supply.

The CCTs are also responsible for ground-based fire control of the AC-130 Spectre gunships and helicopters of AFSOC, as well as for all other air assets, including Army and Navy aircraft. In addition to these capabilities, CCTs provide vital command and control capabilities in the forward area of operations and are qualified in demolition for the removal of obstructions and obstacles in the landing zone or drop zone

Also included under Special Tactics command is the Combat Weather Squadron (CWS). Its mission is to provide meteorological and oceanographic information to the SOF theatre of operations. Their functions include tactical infiltration, data collection, analysis and forecasting, mission tailoring of environmental data, operating jointly with host-nation weather personnel. CWS personnel perform this job from forward-deployed bases or at times from behind enemy lines, using tactical weather equipment and an assortment of communications equipment.

NAVAL SPECIAL WARFARE COMMAND

Navy SEALs

The term SEAL is an acronym for sea, air, and land. Navy SEALs are qualified in diving and parachuting, and are experts at combat swimming, naviga-tion, demolitions, weapons, and many other skills. SEALs operate in small units, or platoons. Squad size is typically eight men with two squads per platoon. In addition to the maritime environment, SEALs also train in the desert, the jungle, in cold weather, and in urban surroundings. Their forte is quick DA raids and they usually are not equipped for long protracted contact with the enemy.

A select group of SEALs are tasked with the operation of the SEAL delivery vehicles (SDVs). These are small submersible craft that allow the SEALs to infiltrate covertly into an enemy harbor or other waterborne target. Should it be necessary to target an Iraqi vessel, gas or oil platform, or other seagoing target, the SEALs would be the first unit of choice.

JOINT SPECIAL OPERATIONS COMMAND (JSOC)

Joint Special Operations Command was created in 1980 as a joint headquarters designated to analyze special operations requirements and techniques and assure interoperability and equipment standardization for SF units. JSOC plans and conducts joint special operations exercises and training, and develops joint special operations tactics. Two units under JSOC are so secret that the Department of Defense does not even acknowledge their existence. These are the Army's Delta Force and Naval Special Warfare Development Group (formerly known as SEAL Team Six). Although each unit has an expansive capability, their primary mission is counterterrorism.

Delta Force

Officially designated as the 1st Special Forces Operational Detachment–Delta (SFOD-D), Delta Force is also is known as the Combat Applications Group (CAG). From its beginnings in 1977, Delta has been heavily influenced by the British Special Air Service (SAS). Subsequently, its current organization mirrors the crack British unit. It is organized into three operating squadrons, all of which (A, B, and C) are subdivided into small groups, or troops. Each troop specializes in high-altitude low-opening (HALO) parachute technique, SCUBA, or other skills. These troops can each be further divided into smaller units as needed to fit mission requirements. Delta also maintains support units, which handle selection and training, logistics, finance, and the unit's medical requirements. Within this grouping is a little known, but vital, technical unit, which is responsible for covert eavesdropping equipment for use in hostage rescues and similar situations.

The vast majority of Delta operators volunteer from the elite Ranger battalions and special forces groups. However, candidates are drawn from all branches of the Army, including the Reserve and National Guard. After the September 11 terrorist attacks, Delta opened the selection to other services, hoping to attract the best possible operators. Their covert and clandestine missions are rarely, if ever de-classified. The mission portrayed in this book's introduction would well be within their realm of expertise.

Naval Special Warfare Development Group (NSWDG)

The Naval Special Warfare Development Group (NSWDG) is responsible for U.S. counterterrorist operations in the maritime environment. The Navy trains counterterrorism operators throughout the U.S. and overseas, both on military and civilian facilities. Organization and manpower of the group is classified, and can only be approximated. It is estimated that NSWDG now numbers somewhere around 200 operators, broken down into teams, much like the British SAS and Delta Force.

These individuals are responsible for the actual testing and development of new Naval Special Warfare equipment, including weapons. NSWDG is reported to be one of only a handful of U.S. units authorized to conduct preemptive actions against terrorists and terrorist facilities.

U.S. MARINE CORPS

Marine Expeditionary Unit –Special Operations Capable (MEU(SOC))

The Marine Corps was not originally included in the command structure of SOCOM upon its creation. However, marines are considered Special Operations Capable forces. When the U.S. Marines deploy into an area, the Marine Expeditionary Unit–Special Operations Capable is proficient in performing special missions and interfacing with traditional SF units.

The MEU(SOC) is a powerful, mobile force, deployable from self-contained floating sea bases. It is uniquely equipped and forward-deployed to respond to any threat, anyplace in the world, within hours. The MEU is made of four elements, command, ground, aviation combat, and service support.

The command element serves as the headquarters for the MEU and allows a single command to exercise control over all ground, aviation, and combat service support forces. The ground combat element (GCE) provides the MEU with its main combat capabilities. The nucleus of the GCE is a marine infantry battalion. The GCE is reinforced for tanks, artillery, amphibious vehicles, engineers, and reconnaissance assets. The aviation combat element (ACE) consists of a composite squadron with transport helicopters such as the CH-46 Sea Knight and CH-53 Sea Stallion, and an armed helicopter, the AH-1W Cobra. In addition to the rotatry wing aircraft, the MEU also has AV-8B Harriers to provide close air support for the marines. Finally, the MEU service support group provides the MEU with mission-essential tasks,

In support of U.S. SOF teams, aircrews and helicopters from the 160th Special Operations Aviation Regiment (Airborne) have been tasked for clandestine insertion, extraction, and re-supply missions. These pilots have been called the best in the world and their ability to operate in the darkness has earned them the nickname, the "Night Stalkers." *USASOC*

U.S. Marines assigned to 2nd Battalion, 2nd Marines, Echo Company, 24th MEU(SOC) disembark from an amphibious assault vehicle (AAV) to conduct a live-fire exercise. Marines from this unit were on a regularly scheduled deployment conducting exercises or missions in CENTCOM's area of responsibility (AOR). *US Navy*

such as medical and dental assistance, motor transport, supply, equipment maintenance, and landing support.

The MEU(SOC) will be composed of approximately 2,000 marines and sailors deployed aboard several amphibious ships. They will make up what is known as an amphibious ready group (ARG). Prior to deployment, the men and women of the MEU will have undergone a rigorous 26-week training program designed to prepare them for any contingency.

Some of the missions MEU (SOC) units are trained for include airfield/port seizures amphibious, raids/assaults/demonstrations, reconnaissance and surveillance, show-of-force operations, seizure/recovery of offshore energy facilities, visit, board, search and seizure of vessels, peacekeeping/enforcement humanitarian/disaster relief, security operations, noncombatant evacuation operations, reinforcement operations and tactical deception operations.

In December 2002, a newly formed Marine Corps SOCOM detachment was formed under the Naval Special Warfare Command. This detachment will be a separate entity from current Marine Force Recon companies. As of this writing, this unit is in the "proof of concept" phase. Thus, chances of their deployment in any Iraq mission would be unlikely.

This detachment will include an HQ element led by a lieutenant colonel and a master gunnery sergeant, both Force Recon marines. It will have a communications section with a handful of Recon communicators, Special Amphibious Reconnaissance corpsmen (SARCs), with one SARC independent duty corpsman (IDC), as well as numerous support people (boat/interim fast-attack vehicle (IFAV) mechanics, riggers etc.), a reinforced Force Recon platoon, and a master sergeant or gunnery sergeant, an Intel detachment consisting of a human intelligence exploitation team (HET), radio reconnaissance team (RRT), and signals intelligence (SIGINT) teams providing SIGINT, electronic intelligence (ELINT) and human intelligence (HUMINT), and a supporting arms liaison team (SALT), otherwise known as an air and naval gunfire liaison company (ANGLICO). The main missions that this detachment is going to be conduct are special reconnaissance, direct action, coalition support, and on a limited scale, foreign internal defense.

CENTRAL INTELLIGENCE AGENCY (CIA)

Special Activities Division (SAD)

Although the Central Intelligence Agency is not part of SOCOM, there is a veiled relationship between the agency's paramilitary and American Special Operations forces. The Special Activities division is one of the least-known covert units operating under NCA control. Highly classified, the SAD is regarded as the preeminent special operations unit in the world. These highly trained and experienced "shadow warriors" are considered to be highly skilled in counterterrorist missions, hostage rescue operations, and "taking down" any type of target, whether vehicle, aircraft, ship, building, or other facility.

SAD is called upon when the president wants to advance U.S. foreign policy in covert ways (i.e., influencing a foreign government without any signs of U.S. involvement). The division also contains the Special Operations Group (SOG), the agency's elite paramilitary cadre. The SOG is divided into ground, maritime, and air branches equipped with light arms, surveillance gear, riverboats, and small planes.

Recently, SAD's shadow warriors have been living up to their highly covert reputation. At a conference commemorating the 60th Anniversary of the CIA's predecessor, the Office of Strategic Services (OSS), CIA Executive Director A.B. Krongard remarked, "Almost sixty years later, in an

Afghan valley, a special forces team—among the first into the country, and itself a proud successor to OSS—ran into a party of mysterious figures. From one of those figures, through a darkness broken only by flashlight, came the roar of an American voice: 'Hi! I'm Hal—damn glad to meet you.' Hal was from the CIA's Special Activities division, and had been scouting the ground, gathering information." Sadly, the first U.S. casualty of Operation Enduring Freedom in Afghanistan was the Special Activities division's Johnny "Mike" Spann.

Air Force Special Operations Command (AFSOC) have brought an assortment of capabilities to the special operations arena. From the large "spectre" gunship to the "pave low helicopters," they have been on call to provide support such as close air support when necessary. In addition to the air assets, AFSOC has also deployed special tactics teams (SSTs) consisting of pararescue jumpers (PJs) and combat control teams (CCTs).CSAR *Defense Visual Information Center*

"The Bear" finds use for "snake eaters"

At the onset of Desert Shield/Desert Storm, General Norman H. Schwarzkopf was apprehensive about deploying U.S. Special Operations forces (SOF). As the Commander-in-Chief (CINC), Central Command, Schwarzkopf came to the theatre of operations carrying a Vietnam-era prejudice. He equated the Green Berets and SEALs to irreverent cowboys who operated outside of the conventional Army standards. He did not care for their type as a young officer in Vietnam. Now, as the man in charge, he intended to keep the "snake eaters" on a short leash.

But the threat of Saddam Hussein attacking Israel forced Schwarzkopf to reconsider. The coalition would also include forces from the Arab nations of the region. Should the Israeli nation enter the war, the Arab alliance would crumble; Arab countries were not willing to fight alongside Israelis. If Saddam could force the Israelis into battle, Schwarzkopf's army would disintegrate before his eyes. In lieu of this definite threat, Schwarzkopf relented, and ordered the insertion of special operations forces into Iraq.

"The Bear," as the burly and no-nonsense commander was affectionately nicknamed, agreed to deploy teams of the 1st Special Forces Operational Detachment–Delta, along with teams from the British Special Air Service. Their mission was to hunt down the elusive Scud missiles and TEL (transport, erector, and launcher) vehicles. Such actions were intrinsic to the overall plan to keep Israel out of the war.

As war plans unfolded, Schwarzkopf studied a multitude of maps, aerial and satellite imagery, and intelligence reports, pondering his next course of action. Again, the skills and expertise of U.S. Special Operations forces came to focus in the eyes of the cynical leader.

Colonel Gary Gray of the 20th Special Operations Squadron was tasked by Schwarzkopf to kick off the air war. A flight of four "Green Hornet" MH-53 Pave Low helicopters would lead an assault force of Army AH-64 Apache helicopters, which would provide the "hammer" for the plan called "Eager Anvil." Once on site, Army Apache pilots would take out

two enemy radar installations simultaneously with AGM-114 Hellfire laser-guided
missiles. The destruction of these radar
sites would open up a corridor for U.S.
and coalition aircraft to begin the air
campaign. Then, as the air war began,
special operations forces teams would
be assigned to behind-the-lines, intelligence-gathering missions.

During Desert Storm, special operations forces conducted deep reconnaissance missions, providing Schwarzkopf
up-to-the-minute intelligence on the
movement of enemy forces. They performed a wide variety of direct action
missions, some which are still classified.
In Iraq and Kuwait, members of this
"elite" brotherhood performed an assortment of missions, which aided in the ultimate success of U.S. and coalition forces.

At the end of the Gulf War, the topic of
U.S. Special Operations forces saw new
life. On one occasion, Schwarzkopf
would comment, "Special forces was the
glue that held the coalition together." It
seemed the Bear had learned the value of
these unconventional warriors.

Navy SEALs bring their expertise in small unit raids
and intelligence gathering, such as sensitive site
exploitation. These waterborne commandos can be
inserted by helicopter, fast-attack vehicle, or SCUBA.
Here, a U.S. Navy lieutenant from SEAL Team Eight
runs down a firing range in Kuwait with an M4A1 and
M203. *Defense Visual Information Center*

Agency SAD teams can range from one-man teams, to twelve-man ODAs, to whole platoons, depending on the mission. Members are the elite of the elite; "the best—period." This results from the sources from which the organization recruits its members: Special Mission units (SMUs); such as Delta Force and NSWDG; SOF units, such as the U.S. Army Special Forces, Navy's SEAL teams, the USMC's Force Reconnaissance units; and from the ranks of the CIA itself.

COMBATING TERRORISM (CBT)

Combating terrorism is a highly specialized, resource-intensive mission. Certain SF units maintain a high state of readiness to conduct CBT operations and possess a full range of CBT capabilities. CBT activities include: antiterrorism, counterterrorism, recovery of hostages or sensitive material from terrorist organizations, attack of terrorist infrastructure, and reduction of vulnerability to terrorism. For some SOF units, counterterrorism is their primary mission. These counterterrorism missions may also be performed by SOF or selected conventional U.S. armed forces under extremely urgent circumstances when principal National Command Authority-designated special operations forces are not readily available (e.g, Combat Applications Group(CAG) or Naval Special Warfare Development Group (NSWDG)).

Force Reconnaissance teams of U.S. Marines may be employed for many tasks, from deep recon, to close air support, to direct action. These highly trained and extremely motivated marines encompass a wide range of special operations capabilities. The fact they are backed up by the full power of a Marine Expeditionary Unit makes them a force to be reckoned with. Here, Force Recon marines of 31st Marine Expeditionary Unit—Special Operations Capable (MEU(SOC)) hone their shooting skills on the aft aircraft elevator of the USS *Essex*. *US Navy*

CHAPTER TWO
MISSION PROFILES

PRINCIPAL MISSIONS

Special operations principal missions fall into nine categories: unconventional warfare, foreign internal defense, special reconnaissance, direct action, combating terrorism, counter-proliferation of weapons of mass destruction, information operations, psychological operations, and civil affairs.

UNCONVENTIONAL WARFARE (UW)

Unconventional warfare is the military and para-military aspect of an insurgency or other armed resistance movement. The focus of UW is primarily on existing or potential insurgent, secessionist, or other resistance movements. Special operations forces provide advice, training, and assistance to existing indigenous resistance organizations. The objective of UW operations is to exploit a hostile power's political, military, economic, and psychological vulnerabilities by advising, assisting, and sustaining resistance forces to accomplish U.S. strategic or operational objectives. UW includes guerrilla warfare, subversion, sabotage, intelligence activities, evasion and escape, and other activities of a low visibility, covert, or clandestine nature. When forces conduct unconventional warfare independently during conflict or war, its primary focus is on political and psychological objectives; when they conduct UW to support conventional military operations, the focus shifts to primarily military objectives.

The recent conditions in Iraq were ripe for introducing UW operations in various regions of the country. From creating a partisan movement, to supporting an internal military takeover, U.S. Special Operations forces were the principal force assigned this task. UW is the bread and butter of the U.S. Army Special Forces; this is the mission they were created to undertake. While special forces groups were originally formed to battle the Soviets during the Cold War, in a sense they have been training for the latest mission for the past fifty years.

The northern territory of Iraq is dotted with isolated encampments, which are home to the Kurds. These people, hated by the Iraqi government, were ideal candidates for a resistance movement against Saddam's

A Kurdish soldier prepares to move out from his mountain encampment. He is armed with an RPG-7, man-portable rocket grenade launcher. As part of their unconventional warfare (UW) mission, Operational Detachment–Alpha were inserted into the northern regions to assist the Kurds in organizing a well-trained resistance force. They learned procedures such as patrolling, raids, and small unit tactics. These partisan forces raised havoc with the Iraqi army units in the area. *Defense Visual Information Center*

regime. For this purpose, covert special forces ODAs were inserted covertly into numerous camps in Kurdish settlements. Here they have supplied the Kurds with weapons, ammunition, and equipment. They also provided food and medical supplies to these forces and their families. The SF teams worked with the Kurds for months to organize them into formidable guerrilla units. Once trained and equipped, these partisans worked with special forces soldiers in performing an assortment of missions against the Iraqi military and infrastructure.

The interaction between special forces and the CIA, specifically the agency's Special Activities division provides another UW scenario. Contact was established with within the Iraqi military, cultivating those individuals interested in supporting a military coup of Saddam's regime.

FOREIGN INTERNAL DEFENSE (FID)

Foreign internal defense involves participation by civilian and military agencies of a government in the actions of another government to free and protect its society from subversion, lawlessness, and insurgency. Special operations forces' primary contribution in this interagency activity is to organize, train, advise, and assist host nation military and

As part of their foreign internal defense (FID) missions, members of the special forces have drawn upon their language skills and cultural training in working with allies around the globe. Here, a group of Kuwait solders from the 15th Brigade, 2nd Infantry Battalion fire M16 rifles on the firing line while being supervised by U.S. Special Forces soldiers. Further instruction will be given on the use and care of the M16 and other weapons. *Defense Visual Information Center*

paramilitary forces. The generic capabilities required for FID include: instructional skills, foreign language proficiency, area and cultural orientation, tactical skills, advanced medical skills, rudimentary construction and engineering skills, familiarity with a wide variety of demolitions, weapons, weapon systems, and communications equipment, and basic psychological operations and civil affairs skills.

Since the end of Desert Storm in 1991, the U.S. has sustained a military presence in and around Iraq, with bases in Kuwait and Saudi Arabia. For example, the 5th Special Force Group (Airborne) maintains a battalion-size force in Kuwait where ODAs are assigned on a rotational basis. For more than a decade these special forces soldiers have been training the Kuwaiti soldiers. Regular training exercises have provided a practical and tactical appreciation of the region by these special operators. These rotational assignments also give the special forces soldiers an opportunity to practice language skills and acclimate to the environment and the culture.

Now that U.S. troops are in Iraq, special operations forces have been supporting the campaign objectives by training, working, and going into combat with the majority of the coalition nations. As in Desert Storm, special operations forces are assigned to each of the coalition units as liaisons between the foreign troops and CENTCOM.

SPECIAL RECONNAISSANCE (SR)

Special operations forces conduct a wide variety of information gathering activities of strategic or operational significance. Special reconnaissance complements national and theatre intelligence collection systems by obtaining specific, well-defined, and time-sensitive information when other systems are constrained by weather, terrain-masking, hostile countermeasures, or conflicting priori-

ties. SR performs human intelligence in hostile, denied, or politically sensitive territories. Special operations forces may carry out these missions unilaterally or in support of conventional operations. Such missions might require advanced reconnaissance and surveillance techniques and equipment, sophisticated clandestine collection methods, and/or the employment of indigenous assets (individuals from the local populace).

Near the city of Mosul in the northern no-fly zone there are eleven regular Iraqi army divisions and two divisions of the Iraqi Republican Guard. It is very probable that SOF teams would do SR on these units. It would be very useful for CENTOM to know such things as the enemy's exact location, strength, equipment, and state of readiness. For such missions, SOF teams would infiltrate near the Iraqi troops to keep watch on their movements. They could accomplish this as mobile patrols "lying up" during the day and patrolling at night, or as small teams hunkered down in a 5-foot by 5-foot hideaway.

Just prior to the start of the war, the U.S. Air Force performed saturation bombing of these forces, obliterating thirteen divisions of Iraqi resistance from northeast of Mosul southwest beyond Kirkuk with B-52 and B-2 bombers. With this opposition neutralized, or at least demoralized into an ineffective fighting force, the Kurds were neatly positioned to carry on a ground attack against the remaining Iraq troops.

DIRECT ACTION (DA)

Direct-action operations are small-scale offensive operations principally undertaken by special operations forces to seize, destroy, capture, recover, or inflict damage on designated personnel or material. In the conduct of these operations, special operations forces may employ raid, ambush, or direct assault tactics; emplace mines and other munitions; conduct standoff attacks by fire from air, ground or

Two members of the 5th Special Forces practice building a hide site in the Nevada desert. Using camouflage netting and indigenous flora, SF teams literally faded into the landscape to perform reconnaissance. When the call comes for special reconnaissance, these SF teams can be on site in a matter of hours. They will carry all the necessary equipment to establish their hide site. During Desert Storm operations, this often meant carrying more than 180 pounds of gear.

maritime platforms; provide terminal guidance for precision weapons; conduct independent sabotage; and perform anti-ship operations.

DA operations are normally limited in scope and duration and usually incorporate a planned withdrawal from the immediate objective area. Special operations forces may conduct these missions unilaterally or in support of conventional operations. DA operations are designed to achieve specific, well-defined, and time-sensitive results of strategic, operational, or critical tactical significance. They frequently occur beyond the reach of tactical weapon systems and selective strike capabilities of conventional forces.

Some military planners thought Saddam might invoke the same scorched earth strategy he tried during Desert Storm. That strategy included blowing up oil wells, setting the countryside ablaze, filling the sky with smoke, and turning the day into darkness. Whether as a diversion or last act of desperation, this would not have been tolerated again

The view from inside a hide site covers a vast area. While an SF team is able to survey a large section of desert from this vantage point, their "hide" is invisible to anyone more than a meter away.

Opposite: Here is an aerial view of a destroyed aircraft hangar in the aftermath of Operation Desert Storm. *Defense Visual Information Center*

A U.S. Marine CH-46 extracts a 1st Force Reconnaissance Company five-man team via a special patrol insertion-extraction (SPIE) rig. *Defense Visual Information Center*

This system is comprised of a Canon digital camera, day and night lenses/image intensifier, lightweight digital image processor, keyboard, modem, and Harris Universal Image transmission software (HUITS). Marines use HUITS for reconnaissance, surveillance, intelligence gathering, and other applications that require real-time imagery and data.

As their name implies, reconnaissance is a skill in which Force Recon marines excel. Here, a marine recon team is inserted by a CH-46 "Sea Knight" helicopter as it begins its mission. These marines may be on site for hours or days, depending on their mission. They are the eyes on target for the MEU(SOC) commander. *Defense Visual Information Center*

by the U.S. and its allies. Before any such action could have come to fruition, teams of Rangers would have assaulted the oil fields and seized control of critical zones. The Rangers would then have secured the area for follow-on forces to establish a security boundary around such compounds.

Bridges and roadways are the primary routes leading into Baghdad. Had they been destroyed it would have caused complications to any approaching army. In similar instances, SOF units might be employed to seize and protect bridges and other critical infrastructure to assure that the fast-rolling juggernaut is not slowed or hindered in any way. Depending on the location and the strength of any defense force protecting the target, this could involve a small commando team or a company of Rangers.

As the January 27, 2003 deadline for disclosure came and went, Hans Blix, the head of the U.N. inspection team, indicated Saddam has not telling the truth concerning Iraq's weapons of mass destruction (WMD). The question was: where were they being stored? While inspection teams roamed from compound to university to other places that might have concealed weapons materials on terra firma, there was the distinct possibility that they were being hidden in a more fluid location— within barges or boats on the Tigris and Euphrates rivers. In similar instances, Navy SEALs might be tasked to perform waterborne infiltration to verify whether such barges exist, and if so, seize and destroy its cargo. Depending on their findings, the SEALs may plant limpet mines on the vessels, or back off and call in air strikes.

Direct action can take a more "personal" approach to expedite regime change. At the time of this writing, it is well within the realm of possibility that Saddam will come under the observation of a very elite member of the special operations forces. From over 800 meters out, armed with an M40A3 or a Barrett M82A1, a sniper team will apply their trade: "one shot—one kill."

COMBATING TERRORISM (CBT)

Combating terrorism is a highly specialized, resource-intensive mission. Certain SOF units maintain a high state of readiness to conduct CBT operations and possess a full range of CBT capabilities. CBT activities include: anti-terrorism (AT), counterterrorism (CT), recovery of hostages or sensitive material from terrorist organizations, attack of terrorist infrastructure, and reduction of vulnerability to terrorism.

COUNTERPROLIFERATION OF WEAPONS OF MASS DESTRUCTION (CP)

Counterproliferation of weapons of mass destruction refers to the actions taken to seize, destroy, render safe, capture, or recover weapons of mass destruction (WMD). SOF units provide unique capabilities to monitor and support compliance with arms control treaties. If directed, SOF units can conduct or support special reconnaissance and direct action missions

Whether called upon to carry out precision direct action raids or help with traditional assaults, members of the special operations community will continue to be involved in urban combat. Each unit trains extensively to hone shooting skills and practice combat in an urban environment. Here, members of the U.S. Army Special Forces practice exiting a building.

A team of Force Reconnaissance marines train in "taking down" a building. The team fast ropes to the roof from a CH-46 helicopter to begin its mission. Assaulting a target in an urban environment such as Baghdad requires speed and aggressive action on target.

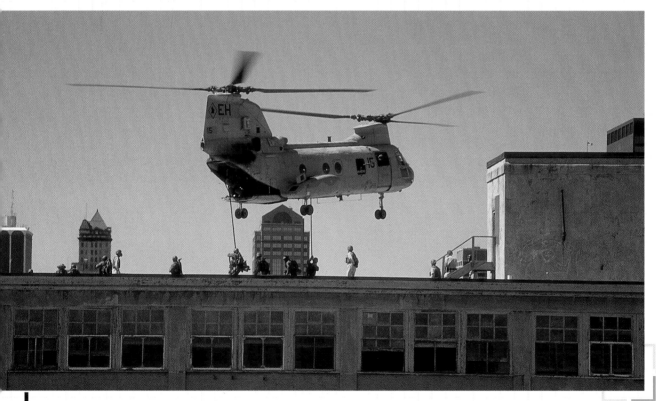

Members of the 75th Ranger Regiment perform an airborne insertion from a U.S. Air Force C-17A Globemaster III. When the mission calls for a large compliment of SOF units on the ground, insertion by parachute is often the best method. The Army Rangers excel in getting a large force on the target, seizing and securing it, and providing security for other SOF units. *USASOC*

The rear view of this close quarters battle (CQB) assault force shows the variety of breaching tools used by the SOF units. These Force Recon marines are carrying (left to right) a power saw, sledge hammer, and hooligan tool. Their assortment of pouches and packs may contain extra ammunition, demolitions, or other mission essential equipment.

"Good to Go!" This marine from the 2nd Force Reconnaissance Company is outfitted with the latest in communications, personal protection, night vision gear, and weaponry. He is wearing an AN/PVS-14 night vision monocular affixed to his helmet and is armed with an M4A1 carbine and an MEU(SOC) 45 as secondary weapon. The M4A1 is equipped with an Aimpoint sight, AN/PEQ-2, Surefire flashlight, and Knight Armament Company suppressor. The heavier welder's gloves attached to a carabineer provide protection during fast-rope insertion.

to locate and interdict sea, land, and air shipments of dangerous materials or weapons. They are tasked with organizing, training, equipping, and otherwise preparing to conduct operations in support of U.S. Government counterproliferation objectives.

INFORMATION OPERATIONS (IO)

Commonly known as "cyber warfare," information operations are actions the military takes to affect adversary information and information systems while defending its own information and information systems. The following activities support the IO mission: direct action, special reconnaissance, psychological operations, and civil affairs.

PSYCHOLOGICAL OPERATIONS (PSYOP)

Psychological operations induce or reinforce foreign attitudes and behaviors favorable to military objectives. It does so by conveying selected information to foreign audiences, meant to influence their emotions, motives, objective reasoning, and ultimately the behavior of foreign governments, organizations, groups, and individuals. Leaflets and radio broadcasts are two common means of conveying this information.

CIVIL AFFAIRS (CA)

Civil affairs missions equate to winning the "hearts and minds" of the people. CA facilitates military operations and consolidates operational activities by assisting commanders in establishing, maintaining,

Navy SEALs disembark an MC-130E Combat Talon, from the 16th Special Operations Wing, Hurlburt Field, Florida, to provide perimeter security for a maintenance team performing critical repairs to an MH-53J Pave Low helicopter at a forward deployed airfield. *Defense Visual Information Center*

influencing, or exploiting relations between military forces and civil authorities, both governmental and non-governmental, and the civilian population in any area of operation, whether friendly, neutral, or hostile.

SOF COLLATERAL ACTIVITIES

SOF's principal missions are enduring and will change infrequently; however, SOF's collateral activities will shift more readily because of the changing international environment. SOF frequently conducts the following collateral activities: coalition support, combat search and rescue, counterdrug activites, countermine activities, humanitarian assistance, security assistance, and special activities.

A U.S. Navy SH-60B Sea Hawk helicopter, loaded with U.S. Navy SEALs, takes off to conduct Maritime Interdiction Operations. The training took place in Kuwait in support of the buildup of U.S. forces in the region. *Defense Visual Information Center*

Military Operations on Urbanized Terrain (MOUT)

Mention urban combat and Rangers recall "the Mog"—Mogadishu, Somali, in October 1993. As depicted in Mark Bowden's book *Black Hawk Down,* and the movie of the same name, the U.S. became involved in an operation that turned into its deadliest firefight since Vietnam. By the end of this mission, eighteen soldiers of Task Force Ranger were dead.

Following this tragic lesson, the U.S. Army Special Forces Command developed its Special Forces Advanced Urban Combat (SFAUC) to specialize in urban terrain, engaging only hostile or theater enemy forces, identifying and engaging targets, breaching and entering buildings, and sophisticated shooting techniques.

The following is an excerpt from the U.S. Army Field Manual regarding MOUT:

CHARACTERISTICS OF
URBAN WARFARE

Constraints on firepower to insure minimum collateral damage within its built-up areas can be expected. Combat operations may be hampered by the presence of civilians in the battle area. Concern for their safety can seriously restrict the combat options open to the commaner.

On the urban battlefield, advantages and disadvantages in the areas of mobility, cover, and observation tend to even out for attacker and defender. Initially, however, the defender has a significant tactical advantage over the attacker because of his knowledge of the terrain.

Unlike deserts, forests, and jungles, which confront the commander with a limited variety of fairly uniform, recurring terrain features, the urban battlefield is composed of an ever-changing mix of natural and manmade features. Frequently, commanders of larger forces will have units fighting on open terrain, on terrain within built-up areas, and on a complex where these two distinct terrain forms merge.

Urban sprawl expands the scope of the commander's terrain analysis and influences the organization and positioning of forces, weapons employment, and maneuver. The dominant role of armor and mechanized infantry on open terrain is balanced by the requirement to fight in that portion of the urban environment, which favors the employment of infantry supported by other arms. Manmade features dispersed in varying densities provide increased cover and concealment while frequently restricting observation and fields of fire. These features are also obstacles to maneuver and are to be avoided by an attacker and used by the defender.

Urbanized terrain normally offers numerous avenues of approach for mounted maneuver well forward of and leading to urban areas. In the proximity of its built-up areas, however, such routes generally become convergent and restrictive. Bypass may be blocked by urban sprawl and the nature of adjacent natural terrain. Avenues of approach within built-up areas are determined by street patterns, building arrangements, open areas, and underground systems. Mounted forces are restricted to streets, alleys, and open areas between buildings. Dismounted forces maximize available cover by moving through buildings and underground systems, along edges of streets, and over roofs.

Weapons employment and target-acquisition ranges are greatly reduced by urban features. On the approaches to urban areas, visibility frequently extends to less than 1,200 meters. Within built-up areas, targets will generally be exposed for brief periods, frequently at ranges of less than 100 meters. These limitations induce close, violent combat between opposing forces, placing great reliance on automatic weapons, rocket launchers, hand grenades, and hand-emplaced high explosives.

Tactical radios, the backbone of command and control networks, will be extremely range-limited within built-up areas.

In possibly no other form of combat are the pressures of battle more intense. Continuous close combat, high casualties, the fleeting nature of targets, and fires from a frequently unseen enemy produce severe psychological strain and physical fatigue particularly among small-unit leaders and soldiers.

A marine sniper team waits on a rocky bluff for the right moment to engage its target. Patience is a virtue among snipers, who wait hours—even days—for the right shot. These highly trained and skilled snipers carry out their mission with the motto "one shot—one kill."

COUNTERDRUG (CD) ACTIVITIES

Counterdrug activities train host nation CD forces on critical skills required to conduct small unit CD operations in order to detect, monitor, and counter the cultivation, production, and trafficking of illegal drugs.

COUNTERMINE (CM) ACTIVITIES

Countermine activities reduce or eliminate the threat to noncombatants and friendly military forces posed y mines, booby-traps, and other explosive devices by training host nation forces in the location, recognition, and safe disposal of mines and other destructive devices, as well as CM program management.

HUMANITARIAN ASSISTANCE (HA)

Humanitarian assistance provides assistance of limited scope and duration to supplement or complement the efforts of host nation civil authorities or agencies to relieve or reduce the results of natural or manmade disasters or other endemic conditions such as human pain, disease, hunger, or privation that might present a serious threat to life or that can result in great damage to, or loss of, property.

SECURITY ASSISTANCE (SA)

Security assistance provides training assistance in support of legislated programs which provide US defense articles, military training, and other defense related services by grant, loan, credit, or cash sales in furtherance of national policies or objectives.

COALITION SUPPORT

Coalition upport integrates coalition units into multinational military operations by training coalition partners on tactics and techniques and providing communications. Coalition support teams often provide the joint force commander (JFC) with an accurate evaluation of the capabilities, location, and activities of coalition forces, thus facilitating JFC command and control.

COMBAT SEARCH AND RESCUE (CSAR)

Combat search and rescue penetrates air defense systems and conducts joint air, ground, and sea operations deep within hostile or denied territory, at night or in adverse weather, to recover distressed personnel. Special operations forces have the natural capability to carry out such missions. There are situations when recovery is beyond the capabilities of component combat rescue forces. Such personnel missions would require SOF units and would resemble direct-action operations, characterized by detailed planning, preparation, rehearsal, and thorough intelligence analysis.

SPECIAL ACTIVITIES

Special activities consist of the planning and execution of actions abroad in support of national foreign policy objectives so that the role of the US government is not apparent or acknowledged publicly. These activities are subject to limitations imposed by executive order and in conjunction with a presidential finding and congressional oversight.

Combat search and rescue (CSAR) missions fall under the responsibility of the SOF units. Here a team of PJs train in extracting a downed pilot from behind enemy lines.
Defense Visual Information Center

CHAPTER THREE

WEAPONS & EQUIPMENT

Special operations forces entered Iraq, covertly and openly, were armed with the latest weaponry and equipment. Over the last decade a number of enhancements have been made to the weapon systems such as the special operations peculiar modification (SOPMOD M4A1) accessory kit. The SOPMOD kit is issued to all U.S. Special Operations forces to expand on the capabilities and operation of the Colt M4A1 carbine. The SOPMOD accessory kit consists of numerous components such as optics, visible and IR lighting systems, in addition to aiming devices that may be attached directly on the M4A1 carbine or to the rail interface system (RIS). The various accessories give the operator the flexibility to choose the appropriate optics, lasers, or lights, dependent on mission parameters.

M4A1 CARBINE

The Colt M4A1 is a more compact version of the full-sized M16A2 rifle. This weapon was

The standard weapon of SOF troops is the M4A1 carbine. The M4A1 is a shortened version of the M16 assault rifle issued to conventional forces. The shorter 14.5-inch barrel and collapsible stock provides the shooter with a compact and versatile weapon. Although the short barrel drops the range of the carbine by approximately 200 meters, the reduced size is an advantage when teams are jammed into the back of helicopters or submarines. The M4A1 is well suited for CQB or CCE, which includes the majority of SOF missions. Unlike the M16A2, the M4A1 does not utilize a three-round burst; instead, the carbine fire selector can be set for safe, semi-automatic or full automatic fire.

The M203 40mm grenade launcher gives the shooters added lethality to the M4A1 carbine. By using multiple arrangements the SOF teams can use concentrated fire by bursting munitions that are extremely useful in raids and ambushes or the ability to illuminate or obscure the target along while simultaneously delivering continuous HEDP fire. The M203 grenade leaf sight attaches to the rail interface system for fire control.

designed specifically for U.S. Special Operations forces. The main difference between the standard M4 and the M4A1 is that the fire selector for the M4 can be selected for semi or three-round burst, while the M4A1 has a fire selection for semi and full automatic operation. The M4A1 is designed for speed of action and lightweight requirements, as is often the case for SOF shooters. The barrel has been redesigned to a shortened 14.5 inches, which reduces weight while maintaining effectiveness for quick-handling field operations. The retractable buttstock has four intermediate stops allowing versatility in close quarters battle (CQB) without compromising shooting capabilities. Such capabilities will be valuable, whether for conducting special raids or for engaging targets in an urban environment.

M203 GRENADE LAUNCHER

The addition of the quick attach/detach M203 mount and leaf sight, combined with the standard

M203 grenade launcher, brings added firepower to the already proven M4A1 carbine for both point and area engagement capability. The most commonly used ammunition is the M406 40mm projectile includes high explosive dual purpose (HEDP). This grenade has a deadly radius of 5 meters, and it used as antipersonnel and anti-light armor. The M433 multipurpose grenade provides fragmentation effects and is capable of penetrating steel armor plate up to 2 inches thick.

meters). As a backup, the ACOG is equipped with an iron sight for rapid close range engagement.

AIMPOINT COMP-M

For close quarters battle, special operations forces have adopted the Aimpoint Comp-M as the standard red dot sighting system.

With both eyes open and head up, the shooter can acquire the target with speed and accuracy. The Comp-M sight superimposes a red dot on the target which the brain sees allowing the soldier to adjust his weapon according when requires in the fast pace shooting environment of CBQ. The Comp-M is parallax free, which means the shooter does not have to compensate for parallax deviation, or apparent change in position of cross hairs as

The receiver of the is made of M203 high strength forged aluminum alloy, providing extreme ruggedness, while keeping the launcher lightweight. A complete self-cocking firing mechanism, including striker, trigger, and positive safety lever is included in the receiver. The barrel is also made of high-strength aluminum alloy, which has been shortened from 12 to 9 inches, allowing improved balance and handling. It slides forward in the receiver to accept a round of ammunition, then slides backward to automatically lock in the closed position, ready to fire.

Carrying out their missions in small teams, SOF operators depend on rapid deployment, mobility and increased firepower, where the emphasis is focused on getting in and out fast.

OPTICS
ADVANCE COMBAT OPTICAL GUNSIGHT (ACOG)

The Trijicon advance combat optical gunsight is the daytime optical scope for the SOPMOD kit. The ACOG is a four-power telescopic sight with a ballistic compensating reticle. Using this reticle increases the capability to direct, identify, and hit targets to the maximum effective range of the M4A1 carbine (600

viewed through an imperfect sighting device. The sight may be mounted on the carrying handle or rail integrated system (RIS) of the M4A1.

HOLOGRAPHIC DISPLAY SIGHT (HDS)

The EOTech holographic display sight, as the name implies, displays holographic patterns. It has been designed for instant target acquisition under any lighting situations, without covering or obscuring the point of aim. The holographic reticle can be seen through the sight, giving the operator a large view of the target or zone of engagement. Unlike other optics, the HDS is passive and gives off no telltale signature. The heads up, rectangular, full view of the HDS eliminates any blind spots, constricted vision or tunnel vision normally associated with cylindrical sights. With both eyes open, the operator sights in on the target for true two-eye operation.

The wide field of view of the HDS allows the operator to sight-in on the target while maintaining peripheral viewing through the sight if needed, up to 35 degrees off axis. A unique feature of the HDS is that it works if the heads-up display window is obstructed by mud, snow, or other elements. Even if the laminated window is shattered, the sight remains fully operational, with the point of aim maintained. The HDS has shown up on many of Delta's weapons and can be used in conjunction with night optical devices (NODs) and night vision goggles (NVGs). The hallmarks of the HDS are speed and ease of use equating incredible accuracy and instant sight on target operation. This can mean the difference between life and death in CQB operations.

ACCESSORIES

AN/PEQ-2 INFRARED ILLUMINATOR/AIMING LASER

The AN/PEQ-2 infrared target pointer/illuminator/aiming laser (ITPIAL) allows the M4A1 to be

The EOTech holographic display sight (HDS) provides a heads-up gun sight especially made for CQB. It is the sight of preference among Delta and DevGru operators fighting throughout the world in undisclosed locales. Its hallmarks are ease of use, incredible accuracy, and instant sight on target operation. These features can be the difference between life and death in such dangerous operations.

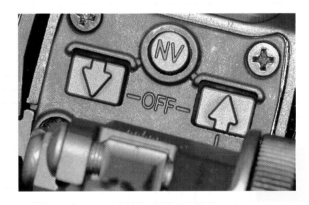

Similar in concept to the Aimpoint sight, the HDS has rectangular optics instead of round, giving the shooter a wider field of view and faster target acquisition.

effectively employed to 300 meters with standard issue night vision goggles or a weapon-mounted night vision device (e.g., the AN/PVS-14). The infrared illuminator, called "Pack-2," broadens the capabilities of NVGs in buildings, tunnels, jungle, overcast, and other low-light conditions, where starlight would not be sufficient to support night vision. It also allows visibility in areas normally in shadow. At close range, a neutral density filter is used to eliminate flare around the aiming laser for improving the view of the target, for identification, and for precision aiming. This combination provides the operator a decisive advantage over an opposing force with little or no night vision capability.

FORWARD HANDGRIP

The forward or vertical handgrip attaches to the bottom of the RIS and provides added support, giving the operator a more stable firing platform. Using the

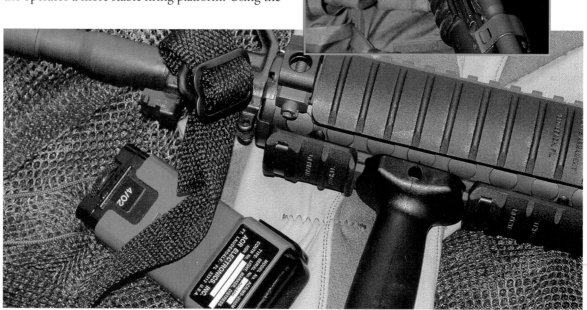

The SOPMOD verical handgrip by Knight Armament Company, fitted to the rail system on an M4. The operator can move the grip forward or back on the rail system to find the most comfortable shooting position.

handgrip brings the shooter's elbows in closer or tighter to his body, consequently keeping the weapon in front of the operator. It provides the operator an efficient method of handling the weapon when additional components have been attached. This provides more precise target acquisition.

QUICK ATTACH SUPPRESSOR

The quick attach/detach (QAD) sound suppressor kit can quickly be attached or removed from the M4A1 carbine. With the suppressor in place, the report of the weapon is reduced by a minimum of 28 decibels (dB). Because the 5.56mm round is supersonic, there will be a "bang," but it is more like a .22-caliber pistol than a 5.56mm round. The suppressor also keeps the muzzle blast to a minimum, assisting the entry team in situation awareness. While the suppressor does not completely eliminate the sound, it does reduce the firing signature (i.e., flash and muzzle blasts). The suppressor is effective as a deceptive measure, interfering with the enemy's ability to locate the shooter and take immediate action. Additionally, it reduces the need for hearing protection during crowded conditions, thus improving inter-team voice communication.

AN/PVS14 NIGHT VISION DEVICE

The AN/PVS-14D is the optimum night vision monocular ensemble for special applications. The monocular or pocket-scope can be hand held, on a facemask, helmet mounted, or attached to a weapon. The new PVS-14D night vision monocular offers the latest, state-of-the-art capability in a package that meets the rigorous demands of special operations forces. The monocular configuration is important to shooters who want to operate with night vision, while maintaining dark adaptation in the opposite eye. The headmount assembly, a standard in the kit, facilitates hands-free operation, when helmet wear is not required. The weapon mount allows for use in a variety of applications from iron sights to red dot or tritium sighting systems, such as the Aimpoint Comp M/ML, Trijicon ACOG system, and EOTech holographic diffraction sight (HDS).

M249 SQUAD AUTOMATIC WEAPON (SAW)

The squad automatic weapon forms the basis of firepower for fire teams. The SAW, or 5.56mm M249, is an individually portable, gas operated, magazine or disintegrating metallic link-belt fed, light machine gun. It has a fixed headspace and quick-change barrel feature and is air cooled, belt fed, and gas operated, firing from the open-bolt position. This automatic weapon has a regulator for selecting either normal (750 rounds per minute

This Force Reconnaissance marine has attached a quick attach/detach sound suppressor kit to an M4A1 carbine. With the suppressor in place, the report of the weapon is reduced by a minimum of 28 decibels (dB). The suppressor also substantially reduces muzzle flash and blast. *Fleet Marine Force Atlantic Combat Camera*

(rpm)) or maximum (1,000 rpm) rate of fire. The M249 engages point targets out to 800 meters, firing the improved NATO standard 5.56mm cartridge. The gunner has the option of using 30-round M16 magazines or linked ammunition from pre-loaded 200-round plastic magazines with the basic load of 600 rounds. The paratrooper or SOF version of the M249 has replaced the fixed stock with a retractable stock and is referred to as the Para-SAW. It is fitted with a rail system for attaching optics, laser, and other devices.

M60E3

Still popular with the Navy SEALs is the M60E3 7.62mm machine gun. Like its predecessor, the M60, this modified version has a lightweight, air-cooled, disintegrating metallic link-belt fed, portable machine gun designed for ground operations. It is gas

Here, a Force Recon marine has transitioned from his M4A1 to an MEU(SOC)-modified M1911A1 .45-caliber handgun. Though the M9 is issued to many SOF units, it is a well-known fact that those who depend on a weapon that delivers accurate stopping power turn to this .45-caliber semi-automatic pistol. It is the weapon of choice among Delta Force operators and is the weapon issued to Marine Force Recon companies. This highly accurate weapon is hand-built by specially trained armorers at the rifle team equipment shop in Quantico, Virginia. The MEU(SOC) 45 is carried as a backup or secondary weapon, dependant on the mission.

The M249 squad assault weapon is an individually portable, air-cooled, belt-fed, gas-operated light machine gun that fires from the open-bolt position. The standard ammunition load is 200 rounds of 5.56mm ammunition in disintegrating belts, alternating four-round full metal jacket, one round tracer. These rounds are fed from a 200-round plastic ammunition box and through the side of the weapon. It has a regulator for selecting either normal 750 rpm or maximum 1,000 rpm rate of fire. It is shown here with an alternate 30-round M16 magazine.

operated with fixed headspace and timing which permits rapid changing of barrels. Differing slightly from the original M60, the M60E3 has a receiver-attached bipod which easily deploys for stability. It has an ambidextrous safety, universal sling attachments, a carrying handle on the barrel, and a simplified gas system. While the original M60 was a crew-served weapon, Navy SEALs consider this an individual weapon. It is not uncommon for the weapon to deliver accurate fire from a shoulder-mounted stance.

M240 MEDIUM MACHINE GUN

The U.S. Army uses the M240B medium machine gun, while the U.S. Marines use the M240G as a replacement for the M60 family of machine guns. Manufactured by Fabrique Nationale, the 24.2-pound M240 medium machine gun is a gas operated, air-cooled, link belt fed weapon that fires 7.62 x 51mm rounds. The weapon fires from an open bolt position. It has a maximum effec-

The M240 is the selected weapon to replace the aging M60 machine gun. The highly reliable 7.62mm machine gun delivers more energy to the target than the smaller caliber M249 squad assault weapon (SAW). It has an effective range of 1.1 miles, with a cyclic rate of fire of 650 to 950 rpm. Shown here a member of the 75th Ranger regiment mans an M240B with a pintle mount on a Ranger special operations vehicle (RSOV). *USASOC*

tive range of 1,100 meters. The rate of fire is adjustable from 750 to 1,400 rpm through an adjustable gas regulator. It features a folding bipod which attaches to the receiver, a quick-change barrel assembly, a feed cover and bolt assembly, enabling closure of the cover regardless of bolt position, a plastic buttstock, and an integral optical sight rail. While is possessed many of the same characteristics as the older M60, the durability of the M240 system results in superior reliability and maintainability.

M24 SNIPER WEAPON SYSTEM (SWS)

The current sniper rifle for U.S. Army Special Forces and Rangers is the M24 sniper weapon system. The M24 is based on the Remington 700 series long action. This action accommodates chambering for either the 7.62 x 51mm or .300 Winchester magnum round. The rifle is a bolt-action six-shot repeating rifle, with one round in the chamber and five additional rounds in the magazine. It is issued with the Leupold Mark IV 10 power M3A scope, commonly referred to as the "Ma-3-Alpha." Additionally, the sniper may make use of its metallic iron sights. Attached to the scope is the M24/EMA anti-reflection device (ARD). Less than 3 inches long, this honeycomb of tubes cuts

A U.S. Navy SEAL, from SEAL Team Eight, maneuvers with an M60 machine gun on a firing range in Kuwait as part of the Southwest Asia buildup. Although more than 40 years old, the M60 has undergone numerous modifications, including shortening the weapon and adding a forward grip. *Defense Visual Information Center*

down the glare of the scope. The M24 SWS comes with a Harris bipod. However, the bipod remains in the deployment case most of the time. The rifle weighs 12.1 pounds without the scope, and is 43 inches long, with a free-floating barrel of 24 inches. The stock is composite Kevlar, graphite, and fiberglass, with an aluminum-bedding block. The stock has an adjustable pad on the buttstock to accommodate the length of pull.

M40A1 Sniper Rifle

The M40A1 was put into service in the 1970s as a long-range sniper rifle. Each rifle is hand built by specially trained and qualified personnel at the Marine Corps Marksmanship Training unit (MTU) at Quantico, Virginia. The M40A1 sniper rifle is based on the Remington model 700, with a heavy barrel, bolt action, five-round magazine fed 7.62mm rifle optimized for accuracy with match grade ammunition. The weapon is equipped with a special Unertl ten-power sniper scope. With the scope, the rifle weighs approximately 14.5 pounds. The unique characteristics of the M40A1 sniper rifle are its commercial competition-grade heavy barrel, McMillan fiberglass stock and butt pad, modified Winchester Model 70 floor plate and trigger guard, and modified and lightened trigger. In addition, each stock is epoxy bedded for accuracy, and all weapons must shoot less than one minute of angle.

M40A3

In 1996, the USMC armorers at Quantico Virginia begin to design the replacement for the

The M24 sniper weapon system (SWS) is the standard issue weapon among Army Rangers and special forces soldiers. Based on a Remington 700 action for 7.62mm, the receiver has been made for adjustment to take the .300 Winchester magnum round. It is equipped with a Leupold Mark IV 10-power fixed scope referred to as the "MA-3 Alpha." A detachable bipod, in this case a Harris, can be attached to the stocks fore-end. The M24 SWS is a bolt-action rifle capable of engaging a target well over 500 meters.

The M40A3 is the latest upgrade to the USMC sniper rifle. The rifles are extremely accurate, very rugged, and are designed from the ground up by USMC armorers at Quantico, Virginia, to be a superb sniper rifle

M40A1, the result was the M40A3. It uses a Remington 700 short action, chambered for 7.62mm NATO, with a steel floor plate assembly and trigger guard built by D.D. Ross. The barrel is Schneider match grade SS#7 and is 24 inches long. The Unertl rings and bases have been replaced with D.D. Ross base and G&G Machine rings. The rifles also come with a Harris bipod and an accessory rail, also built by G&G Machine. The stock is

British soldiers from the Queen's Dragoon Guards and marines from 7th Platoon, 1st Force Reconnaissance Company watch as a British soldier fires an M40A1 sniping rifle *Defense Visual Information Center*

a new McMillan Tactical A4, with adjustable cheek and length of pull.

As the older M40A1s rotate in for service and repair, they are replaced by M40A3s. The rifles are extremely accurate, very rugged, and are designed from the ground up to be a superb sniper rifle. Combined with the new M118LR ammo, it makes a system that is ranked with the best in the world. The magazine capacity for the rifle is five rounds with an effective ranger of 1,000 yards.

M82A1

When the mission calls for a hard target interdiction (HTI) at very long range (i.e., over 1,000 meters) SOF teams will turn to the big guns. HTI can take out such targets as a generators, airplanes, helicopters, or other vehicles. The M82A1 is a one-man portable, semi-automatic rifle with a magazine holding up to ten rounds of .50 caliber, Browning Machine Gun (BMG) ammunition. Other features include a quick-detachable bipod with spiked feet, iron sights, and an M1913 (Picatinny) optical rail to accommodate various sighting and aiming devices.

M3 CARL GUSTAV

Manufactured by Bofors of Sweden, the M3 multi-role anti-armor anti-personnel weapon system (MAAWS) is popular with the Rangers, and has gained favor with the SEALs. The M3 consists of the Carl Gustaf rifle and an assortment of 84mm ammunition. The variety of ammunition includes high explosive (HE), high explosive antitank (HEAT), high explosive dual purpose (HEDP), smoke, illumination, target practice (TP) and sub-caliber adapter training systems. The effective range varies from 200 to 1,300 meters, depending on the ammunition type. The M3 Rifle weighs approximately 25 pounds and is 42 inches long. It uses a Picatinny fire

A marine from 7th Platoon, 1st Force Reconnaissance Company prepares to fire an AT-4 light anti-tank weapon while taking part in a training exercise in the Persian Gulf. The M136 AT-4 is a lightweight, self-contained, man-portable, anti-armor weapon. Inside of the expendable, one-piece fiberglass-wrapped tube is a free-flight, fin-stabilized, rocket-type cartridge. *Defense Visual Information Center*

Smoke drifts away from a target hit by an AT-4 round. *Defense Visual Information Center*

A U.S. Navy Corpsman in the 26th MEU(SOC) waits with his Barrett M82A1 rifle on the flight line prior to boarding a Marine Corps KC-130. The marines refer to the Barrett as the special application scoped rifle (SASR). *Defense Visual Information Center*

The M3 Carl Gustav weapons system has become a preferred anti-armor weapon with SOF units, especially Rangers and SEALs. The M3 fires a wide variety of ammunition and is well suited for both desert as well as urban warfare. Whether encountering a Republican Guard MBT on the wide Iraqi expanse or a BMP on the streets of Baghdad, SOF operators find the M3 a valued asset. *USASOC*

Opposite: The SOFLAM, or what its manufacturer calls the ground laser target designator (GLTD II), is a compact, light-weight, portable laser target designator and rangefinder. The SOFLAM is capable of exporting range data via an RS422 link and importing azimuth and elevation. It was designed to enable special operations forces to direct laser-guided smart weapons, such as Paveway bombs, Hellfire missiles, and Copperhead munitions. The AN/PEQ-1A would be part of a sophisticated, digitized fire control system with thermal or image-intensified sights.

control device (PFCD) as a mount for optical/night sights. It addresses trajectory differences between HEAT, HE, and HEDP rounds.

AT4

The M136 AT4 is the Army's principal light anti-tank weapon, providing precision delivery of an 84mm high explosive anti-armor warhead, with negligible recoil. The M136 AT4 is a man-portable, self-contained anti-armor weapon consisting of a free flight, fin-stabilized, rocket-type cartridge packed in an expendable, one-piece, fiberglass-wrapped tube. Unlike the M72 LAW, the AT4 launcher does not need to be extended before firing. When the warhead makes impact with the target the nose cone crushes and an impact sensor activates the internal fuse. Upon ignition, the piezoelectric fuse element triggers the detonator, initiating the main charge. This result is penetration with the main charge firing and sending the warhead body into a directional gas jet capable of penetrating more than 17 inches of armor plate. This results in the spalling

(splitting off) and projecting of fragments and incendiary effects, the generation of blinding light, and obliteration of the interior of the target.

AN/PEQ-1A SOFLAM

The AN/PEQ-1A special operations forces laser acquisition marker (SOFLAM) is used in a direct action mission for the direction of terminal guided ordnance (TGO), or lasing the target. This newly issued laser-marking device is lighter and more compact than the current laser marker in service with the U.S. military. It provides the operators with the capability to locate and designate critical enemy targets for destruction using laser-guided ordinance. It can be employed in daylight or at night with the attached night vision optics.

GLOBAL POSITIONING SYSTEM (GPS)

While all SOF operators excel in land navigation using the standard issue lensatic compass, pinpoint accuracy is equally important when teams conduct

Marines from the 2nd Force Reconnaissance Company, 26th MEU(SOC) seen here with an AN/PEQ-1A special operations forces–laser acquisition marker (SOFLAM). The SOFLAM is used to guide smart bombs to their designated target. During Operation Enduring Freedom, Saddam Hussein positioned many of his military assets in close proximity of school, hospitals, and mosques. To limit the amount of collateral damage, SOF teams equipped with SOFLAM equipment would provide the means to carry out surgical strikes.

direct action missions through the desert, or across the frozen tundra, in enemy territory, or in the middle of the night. They need to know the position of terrorist compounds, radar stations, or Scuds when reporting into headquarters. For such instances they will use a global positioning system.

GPS uses a collection of satellites that orbit the Earth twice a day. During this orbiting they transmit precise time, latitude, longitude, and altitude information. Using a GPS receiver, special operations forces can ascertain their exact location anywhere on Earth.

GPS was developed by the U.S. Department of Defense in the early 1970s to provide continuous worldwide positioning and navigating for U.S. military forces around the globe. The complete "constellation" of air force NAVSTAR global positioning system consists of twenty-four satellites orbiting approximately 12,000 miles above the Earth. These twenty-two active and two reserve satellites provide data 24 hours a day for two- and three-dimensional positioning anywhere on the planet. Each satellite continuously broadcasts precise time and location data.

Troops using a GPS receiver receive these signals. GPS satellites orbit the Earth every 12 hours,

An aviation ordnanceman applies the final wiring to a GBU-24, 200-pound laser guide bomb attached to an F-14 Tomcat. The GBU-24 low-level laser-guided bomb (LLLGB) consists of either a 2,000-pound MK-84 general-purpose bomb or BLU-109 penetrator bomb modified with a Paveway III low-level laser-guided bomb kit to add the proportional guidance. The GBU-24 is designed for low-altitude delivery and greater standoff ranges for reduced exposure. The weapon has low-level standoff capability of more than 10 nautical miles. *Defense Visual Information Center*

The joint direct attack munition (JDAM) is based on a BLU-109 2,000-pound bomb. An Air Force weapons loader preps a JDAM for loading into a B-1 Lancer bomber. The B-1 can hold 24 of these bombs in its three bomb bays. The JDAM is a guidance tail kit that converts conventional free-fall bombs into accurate "smart" bombs. The tail kit contains a global positioning and inertial navigation system, autonomously navigating to its target to provide surgical strikes in any type of weather conditions, day or night. *Defense Visual Information Center*

An F-117 Nighthawk engages its target and drops a GBU-28 guided bomb unit. The GBU-28 is a special weapon developed for penetrating hardened Iraqi command centers located deep underground. This 5,000-pound laser-guided conventional munition uses a 4,400-pound penetrating warhead. The bombs are modified Army artillery tubes, weighing 4,637 pounds and containing 630 pounds of high explosives. They are fitted with GBU-27 laser-guided bomb (LGB) kits, are 14.5 inches in diameter, and are almost 19 feet long. The operator illuminates a target with a laser designator, guiding the munition to a spot of laser energy reflected from the target. It is capable of penetrating 100 feet of ground or 20 feet of concrete. *Defense Visual Information Center*

emitting continuous navigation signals on two different L-band frequencies. The signals figure time to within a millionth of a second, velocity to within a fraction of a mile per hour, and location to within meters. Positioning accuracy for military users is normally 16 meters

By measuring the time interval of the transmission and the receiving of the satellite signal, the GPS receiver calculates the distance between the users and each satellite. Using the distance measurements of at least three satellites in an algorithm computation the GPS receiver provides precise location. A precise positioning service (PPS), which is used by the military, uses a special encryption signal. A second signal, called a standard positioning service (SPS), is available for civilian and commercial use.

The current GPS unit is Rockwell's precise lightweight GPS receiver (PLGR96), often referred to as "plugger." This hand-held GPS unit addresses the ever-increasing demands of U.S. Special Operations forces.

Secure (Y-code) differential GPS (SDGPS) is accurate to wo within 1 meter. Other features of the "plugger" include wide-area GPS enhancement

The BLU-82B/C-130 weapon system, nicknamed the "Daisy Cutter," is a high-altitude delivery, 15,000-pound conventional bomb. This bomb's size and weight necessitates delivery from an MC-130. It is the largest conventional muniton in the U.S. inventory. Yet, it is so powerful that during deployment in Desert Storm, excited members of the British SAS reported back to headquarters, "The Americans are using nukes!" The warhead contains 12,600 pounds of a mixture of ammonium nitrate, aluminum powder, and polystyrene, and it is detonated just above ground level by a 38-inch fuse extender. The weapon produces an overpressure of 1,000 pounds per square inch near ground zero. *USAF*

The Rockwell precise lightweight GPS receiver (PLGR96), commonly referred to as "plugger," will continuously track up to five satellites. The unit is sealed for operations in all environments, and accurately computes position coordinates, elevation, speed, and time data transmitted from Navstar GPS satellite signals.

(WAGE) for auto-nomous positioning accuracy to within 4 meters, jammer direction finding, targeting interface with laser range-finder, remote display terminal capability, and advanced user interface features.

Weighing a mere 2.7 pounds (with batteries installed), this GPS unit is easily stowed in a cavernous rucksack or even in the pocket of an assault vest. In addition to hand-held operation the PLGR96 unit can be installed into various vehicles and airborne platforms.

In addition to the PLGR, a large number of the SOF teams have obtained commercial GPS units, such as the Garmin 12 or eTrex. These newer consumer systems have the latest technology, allowing them to acquire the satellite even faster than the older Department of Defense (DOD) units.

GMV (GROUND MOBILITY VEHICLE)

The ground mobility vehicle has its origins in Desert Storm. During the Gulf War, special operations forces modified the "Humvee" for extended desert missions, and dubbed it the "Dumvee." The modifications included heavier suspension, a more powerful engine, an open bed, and back for storage of water and fuel and other mission-essential items. The GMV is designed for use over all types of roads, in all weather conditions, and are extremely effective in the most difficult terrain. It is equipped with a winch and fitted with a brush guard. The vehicle's high power-to-weight ratio, four-wheel drive, and high ground clearance combine to give it outstanding cross-country mobility. It has a towing capacity of 4,200 pounds with a cruising range of 275 miles.

Used by SF mounted teams, the basic team makeup is four GMVs per team, with a crew of three men per vehicle. The GMV greatly enhanced the capability of mounted ODAs, extending their mission endurance and flexibility. The GMV has a cupola on top, similar to that used for mounting a tow system. It is used for mounting various weapons systems, such as the M2, .50-caliber machine gun and Mark 19, 40mm machine grenade launcher.

Members of special forces mobility teams are taught how to drive the GMV safely and effectively at special schools such as Rod Hall Advanced Military Off-Road Driver Training in the desert of Nevada. The SF soldiers learn techniques such as brake modulation, which allows them to work the ups and downs of the harsh desert envi-

The ground mobility vehicle (GMV) had its origins in Desert Storm. The GMV has a cupola on top, similar to that used for mounting a tow system, for mounting various weapons systems such as the M2 .50-caliber machine gun and Mark 19, 40mm machine grenade launcher.

ronment, and navigate over rocking, uneven terrain. The soldiers also learn how to maintain the vehicle and make necessary repairs in the field.

RANGER SPECIAL OPERATIONS VEHICLE (RSOV)

The Ranger special operations vehicle is based on the Land Rover Defender Model 110. Currently used by the 75th Rangers in multiple variants, the RSOV provides the Rangers with a multipurpose tactical transport for moving Rangers and their equipment in a variety of operational environments.

A special forces GMV armed with a .50-caliber heavy machine gun provides SF soldiers with considerable firepower to engage enemy forces.

A member of the 5th Special Forces Group (Airborne) loads a Mark 19, 40mm grenade machine gun with linked 40mm grenades. The Mark 19 is a self-powered, air-cooled, belt-fed, blow-back operated weapon. The MK19 is designed to deliver accurate, intense, and decisive firepower against enemy personnel and lightly armored vehicles.

Below: "DUMMV" was the name given to a modified version of the HUMMV used for desert operations during Desert Shield/Storm. This ultimate 4x4 vehicle allows SF soldiers to execute missions at long range or serve as a mission support site (MSS), from which ODAs have operated out of their area of operations. This particular GMV is armed with a Mark 19, 40mm grenade machine gun, and is loaded with fuel cans, water, ammunition, and other mission-essential equipment. Attached to the rear of the vehicle is camouflage netting that may be deployed by the team to conceal their MSS.

Members of the 5th Special Forces, ODA-581 deploy camouflage netting over their DUMMVs. Once the two vehicles have been concealed in this manner, they will blend in with the environment. This MSS will serve as a resupply base and radio relay point for dismounted patrols.

The RSOV is fitted with a weapon mount to accommodate, an MK19, M2, .50-caliber main weapon or M60/M240G machine gun. Anti-armor capabilities are provided by M3, 84mm Carl Gustav recoilless rifle, Javelin, AT-4 or light antitank weapons. For air threats, Stinger (shoulder-launched surface-to-air) missiles can be placed in the stowage rack. It is also common to see a 60mm mortar strapped to the fender. Although the RSOV is bristling with weapons, the vehicle is primarily for transport, not for use as a fighting platform.

A fully loaded-out vehicle weighs approximately 7,734 pounds. The wheelbase is 110 inches, and with an overall length of 174 inches, width of 70.5 inches, and height of 76 inches (without weapon mount). It fits into both the 160th SOAR MH-47 and AFSOC MH-53 helicopters. Additionally, any tactical cargo transport aircraft in the U.S. Air Force inventory can transport the RSOV.

With a ground clearance of 10 inches, grade of 45 degrees, and capable of traversing 30 degrees,

the RSOV is as at home in the desert as it is in the urban environment. It is powered by a four-cylinder inter-cooled turbocharged diesel engine, affording a fully loaded RSOV with a range of 200 miles. Carrying extra fuel in five-gallon cans will extend this range even more. Placed in and around the vehicle are multiple stowage and straps, concertina mounts, and lashing points. It is also fitted with a 7,000-pound-capacity winch.

The standard crew for an RSOV consists of a driver/team leader, a truck commander and a gunner. Depending on mission parameters, the vehicle can accommodate up to seven Rangers. Augmentation to the normal crew may include an antitank gunner, radiotelephone operator (RTO), or a dismount team. The seating arrangement of the RSOV positions the Rangers facing out in all directions, giving them an unrestricted, omnidirectional view.

There are two variants to the RSOV. One is the medical special operations vehicle (MEDSOV), and the other is the mortar special operations vehi-

Each Ranger battalion possesses 12 Ranger special operations vehicles, which are ideal for airfield seizure. The vehicle, based on the Land Rover Defender Model 110, provides the Rangers with a multipurpose tactical transportation and weapons platform capable of moving Rangers and their equipment through an assortment of environments. *USASOC*

cle (MORTSOV). The MEDSOV replaces the weapon mount with fold-down rack capable of holding six litters. Each Ranger battalion will have two of these vehicles with a crew that includes a driver, a truck commander, and two or three medics to treat the wounded. The MORTSOV replaces the weapon mount with storage boxes. This modifications allows the vehicle to carry thirty 120mm mortar rounds along with the extra equipment required by the platoon. In addition to its onboard carrying capacity, the MORTSOV can be used to tow the platoon's 120mm mortars. There are two of these vehicles per each Ranger battalion.

FAST-ATTACK VEHICLE (FAV)

Both Delta Force and the SEALs use fast-attack vehicles, though the Navy calls them desert patrol vehicles. Manufactured by Chenowth in El Cajon, California, these hybrid dune buggies can drive faster than motorcycles and go places even a Humvee would fear to tred.

The frame is polyfiber and the cowling can be removed dependent upon the mission. Baskets alongside the frame have multiple uses. They can be used for storage of food, water, ammunition, and gear. Collapsible fuel bladders can also be mounted in the baskets, giving the FAV an extended range for special missions. The baskets can also be used for the recovery of personnel.

The engine is a 4-cylinder air-cooled motor with an internal/external oil cooler. This is a big improvement over the FAVs used in Desert Storm. With the new oil cooler, it runs wide open in over 120-degree weather with no problems. The air cleaner is a two-stage system. Regardless of the conditions, the first stage filters all the dirt before it reaches the second stage of the air cleaner.

Clearance is approximately 16 inches, with 24 inches of wheel travel. It has four shocks in the rear, with three working constantly and the fourth as a secondary shock. When the rear wheel travels a certain distance, it engages an additional set of torsion bars and the fourth shock. The entire vehicle is tunable by the crew dependent on mission, load and terrain. It can carry 2,000 pounds of gear. The seats feature five-point harnesses, so the tighter the strap, the better the comfort.

Micky Thompson Beadlock tires allow the vehicle to continue to maneuver even with flat tires. The sidewall also features a tread pattern there will be traction regardless of inflation. The FAV features cutting-brakes along with disc brakes. By operating levers, the driver can brake the vehicle and place it in a sharp turn. This is extremely useful in an ambush when the driver needs to maneuver the vehicle to line armament up on an enemy.

The vehicle has a number of hard points to mount various weapons systems. There are two racks for AT-4s (antitank missiles), and an addi-tional AT-4 can be carried in the side baskets. The baskets can also hold Stingers. The top mount will accept a M2, .50-caliber machine gun or Mark 19, 40mm grenade launcher. The front mount for the operator riding "shotgun" accepts a 7.62mm light machine gun (e.g., M60E3 or M240). The Mark 19, 40mm machine grenade launcher can also be mounted on the vehicle, which gives the crew substantial firepower. There is also a rear mount for an

A right front view of a desert patrol vehicle (DPV) during training exercise on the Silver Strand at Coronado. The DPV is a three-man vehicle used for many long-range desert operations including close air support or combat search and rescue missions. The vehicle is armed with a variety of weapons, including the Browning .50-caliber heavy machine gun, the Mark 19, 40mm grenade launcher; and the M60 .30-caliber machine gun. *Defense Visual Information Center*

Stowage and configuration features include an MK19 or .50-caliber main weapon, M60/M240G mount, Stinger missile stowage rack, multiple storage compartments and straps, concertina mounts, vehicle lashing points, and a 7,000-pound-capacity winch. Anti-armor capabilities include the M3, 84mm Carl Gustav rifle, javelin, AT-4, and light antitank weapons. *USASOC*

A U.S. Navy SEAL performs a live-fire target shooting exercise from the back seat of a DPV. He is using an M2 .50-caliber heavy machine gun, mounted with an AN/PEQ-2 IR laser pointer for nocturnal missions. In the foreground is a light anti-armor weapon. *US Navy*

M60E3 or other light machine gun, useful when breaking contact with enemy forces.

INTERIM FAST-ATTACK VEHICLES (IFAV)

The Marine Corps' interim fast-attack vehicle (IFAV) is based on the Mercedes-Benz MB 290 GD 1.5 ton off-road Wolf model manufactured for the German Bundeswehr. According to Marc Stanley, president of Advance Vehicle Systems, which is partnered with Daimler Chrysler on the project, "The M1511 IFAV is a tactical vehicle designed for use over all types of roads, as well as cross-country terrain in all weather conditions." The IFAV can ford up to thirty inches of water, has a climbing ability of 80 percent, and can tow up to 7,700 pounds.

Inside a desert patrol vehicle (DPV) of SEAL Team Three during a training exercise at the Naval Amiles per Houribious Base are Lieutenant Junior Grade Thomas Chaby (right) and Hospital Corpsman First Class Joe Pappamihiel. They have access to an arsenal of weapons, including the Browning .50-caliber heavy machine gun and the Mark 19 grenade launcher. *Defense Visual Information Center*

The IFAV is powered by a 2.9-liter turbocharged, intercooled diesel engine, providing an acceleration of 0 to 60 miles per hour in 17 seconds, with a top speed of 97 miles per hour. The vehicle entered into service with the U.S. Marines in 1999 as a replacement to the aging M151 Jeep fast-attack vehicle, as well as the light strike vehicle (LSV), the "sister" vehicle to the desert patrol vehicle (DPV).

The interim fast-attack vehicle (IFAV) is a compact military SUV with a range well over 300 miles, a maximum road speed of 96 miles per hour, and an estimated fuel consumption of 18 miles per gallon. It can ford water to a depth of 30 inches, making it suitable for Marine Corps operations.

Marines deployed IFAVs with MEU(SOC) units during Operation Enduring Freedom. Force Reconnaissance teams used IFAVs to perform long-range, deep-penetration recon missions in Iraq. *Fleet Marine Force Atlantic Combat Camera*

Right: Here, members of the 2nd Force Reconnaissance Company from Camp LeJeune put the IFAV through its paces during desert training. The normal IFAV crew consist of a team leader, a driver, a gunner, and an assistant gunner. The vehicle will take a wide assortment of weapons, including the M240G, MK19, 40mm grenade cannon, and M2 .50-caliber machine gun. *Courtesy 2nd Force Recon*

Deep behind enemy lines, a Force Reconnaissance team performs an insertion with an IFAV transported by a CH-53 helicopter. Weighing in at 7,760 pounds with an overall length of 180 inches and width of 63.5 inches, it easily fits into the helicopter's cargo bay. IFAVs also are capable of being transported by MV-22 Ospreys. *USMC*

The design and size of the IFAV permits it to be carried inside of current Marine Corps rotary aircraft (e.g., CH-46 Sea Knight and CH-53 Sea Stallion helicopters). Unlike the former LSV/DPV the IFAV will fit into the CV-22 Osprey, giving the marines a mobile platform for future operations. Additionally, it can be parachute-dropped behind enemy lines by aircraft taking off from forward deployed Navy ships.

The vehicle will carry up to six marines and their gear, dependent on mission parameters. It is equipped with a 9,000-pound Warn electric winch. The IFAV is fitted with a pedestal mount, which can accommodate an M230G 7.62mm machine

In comparison to the Flyer II (foreground), the Flyer internally transportable vehicle (ITV) is 14 inches narrower, allowing the vehicle to be transported in the CV-22 Opsrey tilt-rotor aircraft. It has a ground clearance of 10 to 18 inches and supports a wide assortment of armament. *Flyer Technologies*

A Flyer II is loaded into the cargo bay of a CH-53 Sea Stallion. Powered by a rear-mounted VM 429 DOHC turbocharged intercooled diesel, the vehicle can reach speeds of up to 75 miles per hour. It features four-wheel independent suspension and is equipped with a 10,000-pound wench. It can accommodate up to five passengers. *Flyer Technologies*

gun; a Mark 19, 40mm.machine grenade launcher; an M2, .50-caliber machine gun; or tube-launched, optically tracked, wire-guided (TOW) missile launcher. There is also cargo space to store a couple of AT-4s as well as hang points for attaching the team's rucksacks or other kit.

The IFAV has been combat tested by members of 2nd Platoon, 1st Force Recon Company, for mobile reconnaissance, raids, and interdiction in southern Afghanistan in support of Operation Enduring Freedom. It is sure to get a similar work-out in the deserts of Iraq and the streets of Baghdad.

CHAPTER FIVE

AIR ASSETS

FIXED WING AIRCRAFT
AC-130U SPECTRE GUNSHIP

The primary mission of the AC-130U is to deliver precision firepower in support of close air support for special operations and conventional ground forces. The Spectre can provide accurate fire support with limited collateral damage, and can remain on station for extended periods of time.

The lethality of this gunship is found in three weapon systems located on the port or left side of the fuselage. In the front section of the aircraft, just right of the crew hatch, is the GAU-12/U 25mm Gatling cannon. This weapon is full traversable, capable of firing 1,800 rpm from altitudes of 12,000 feet. Located further back on the gunship, just aft of the landing gear, is the 40mm Bofors gun and the 105mm Howitzer cannon. The 40mm is well suited for firing in situations of "danger close" support (support in close proximity to friendly forces) due to its small fragmentation pattern. Alongside the Bofors is the M102, 105mm Howitzer cannon, a by-product of the U.S. Army M1A1 howitzer, which has been modified to fire from an aircraft.

The flagship of AFSOC is the AC-130 U-model gunship. The AC-130 gunship's primary missions are close air support, air interdiction, and force protection. Close air support missions include troops in contact, convoy escort, and urban operations. Air interdiction missions are conducted against preplanned targets or targets of opportunity. Force protection missions include air base defense and facilities defense. *USAF*

Unlike the "fast movers" (e.g. F-15s, A-10s etc.) which require qualified forward air controllers (FAC) for ordinance delivery in danger close support, the AC-130U can be controlled by fire support officers, team leaders or self-forward air controllers (FACs). The fire control officers are located in the battle management center (BMC). Here they man the state-of-the-art sensors, navigation and fire control systems. Additionally, the BMC is equipped with night vision and thermal imaging systems enabling the Spectre to mete out death in total darkness. These systems, cou-

pled with the trained eyes and skilled hands of its officers, enable the crew to deliver the gunship's firepower with surgical precision, or for area saturation, even in adverse weather conditions.

MC-130E/H COMBAT TALON

The MC-130E Combat Talon I and the MC-130H Combat Talon II are designed for long-range clandestine or covert delivery of special operations forces and equipment. It provides global, day, night, adverse-weather, air-drop, and air-land personnel

The GAU-12/U 25mm Gatling cannon is fully traversable and capable of firing 1,800 rpm. This weapon can track on target as the aft weapons array targets another, operating from extended altitudes of 12,000 feet.

Right: Gunners load ammunition into the Bofors 40mm cannon. The 40mm ammo comes in stacks of four per pack and can be continuously fed into the weapon as it fires.

and equipment capabilities in support of U.S. and allied special operation forces.

Combat Talons are equipped with forward-looking infrared radar, which provides an infrared image of terrain features, ground and airborne objects, terrain following/avoidance radars, and specialized aerial delivery equipment. Incorporated into the Talons is a fully integrated inertial navigation (IIN), global positioning system (GPS), and high-speed aerial delivery system. The Talons use infrared flight rules (IFR), which means the aircraft

can be used in heavy ground fog or low cloud cover, when the pilots cannot see the ground and must depend on instruments.

These special navigation and aerial delivery systems are used to locate small drop zones and deliver personnel or equipment with greater accuracy and at higher speeds than possible with a C-130. Such an example would be the insertion of an SOF team operating in sensitive or hostile territory. MC-130E/H Combat Talons are able to penetrate hostile airspace at low altitudes to carry out these

Spectre gunners prepare the 105mm howitzer cannon for firing. As they load the weapon, the fire control officer in the battle management center of the aircraft is using sophisticated monitors, thermal imagers, surveillance, and other devices to pinpoint their next target.

Below: Here is a night vision view from the flight deck of an MC-130E Combat Talon during a nighttime operation mission. The 16th Special Operations Wing is deployed to the Joint Special Operation Aviation Component South at a classified location in support of the global war on terrorism. *Defense Visual Information Center*

missions. Talon crews are specially trained in night and adverse weather operations.

MC-130P
COMBAT SHADOW

The MC-130P, or Combat Shadow, extends the range of special operations helicopters, such as the 160th SOAR(A) or AFSOC assets, by providing air refueling. Operations are conducted primarily in formation, at night, and at low-level to reduce the probability of visual acquisition and intercept by airborne threats. This is carried out in clandestine, low visibility, and low-level missions into politically sensitive or hostile territory. The MC-130P may fly in a single or multi-ship mission to reduce detection.

The secondary mission of the Combat Shadow includes the delivery of SOF operators. Small teams, assorted gear, equipment, Zodiacs and combat rubber raiding craft (CRRC) are a few of the specialized items that are conveyed by the aircraft and its crew. The Shadow is a visual flight rule (VFR) aircraft and would be used when the pilots can see the ground. Penetrations will often use radar. Incorporated into this aircraft, the Combat Shadow has fully integrated inertial navigation (IIN), GPS, and both interior and exterior night-vision goggle-compatible lighting. This allows the crew to use an NVG-compatible heads-up display (HUD) to fly the plane. It has a forward-

The mission of the MC-130E Combat Talon I and MC-130H Combat Talon II is to provide global, day, night, and adverse weather capability to airdrop and air-land personnel and equipment in support of U.S. and Allied special operations forces. These aircraft are equipped with in-flight refueling equipment, terrain-following, terrain-avoidance radar, an inertial and global positioning satellite navigation system, and a high-speed aerial delivery system. The special navigation and aerial delivery systems are used to locate small drop zones and to deliver people or equipment with greater accuracy and at higher speeds than the standard C-130. The aircraft is able to penetrate hostile airspace at low altitudes, while crews are trained for night and adverse weather operations. *USAF*

The MC-130P flies clandestine, low visibility, low-level missions into politically sensitive or hostile territory to provide air refueling for special operation helicopters. The MC-130P primarily flies its single- or multi-ship missions at night to reduce detection and intercept by airborne threats. Secondary mission capabilities include airdrop of small special operations teams, small bundles, and zodiac and combat rubber raiding craft, as well as night-vision goggle takeoffs and landings, tactical airborne radar approaches, and in-flight refueling as a receiver. *USAF*

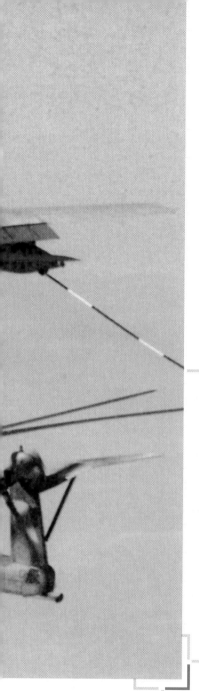

The primary mission of the EC-130 Commando Solo is to conduct psychological operations, civil affairs broadcast missions, and electronic countermeasures. The EC-130 is not only capable of jamming enemy signals and communications but also pinpointing attempts to jam communications by the enemy in an electronic environment. The crew of the Commando Solo can carry out its PSYWAR mission day or night. *Defense Visual Information Center*

looking infrared radar, missile and radar warning receiver to alert the crew of threats. Countermeasure devices include chaff and flare dispensers. Communications will have satellite and data burst technology. In addition, the MC-130P will have in-flight re-fueling capability as a receiver.

ROTORY WING AIRCRAFT
MH-53M PAVE LOW III E

The mission of the MH-53M is carry out low-level, long-range, undetected flights into denied or hostile areas. This is accomplished day or night, even under the worst weather conditions, for infiltration, exfiltration, and re-supply of special operations forces. Equipped with forward-looking infrared, inertial GPS, Doppler navigation systems, terrain-following/avoidance radars, on-board computer, and integrated advanced avionics, it achieves precise, low-level, long-range penetration into denied areas, day or night, in adverse weather and over hazardous terrain without detection.

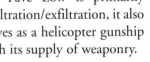

MH-53M Pave Low is equipped with an interactive defensive avionics system/multi-mission advanced tactical terminal (IDAS/MATT). This modification provides air crews with a heighten level of readiness and efficiency. This system is a color, multifunctional, night-vision-compatible digital map screen. Located on the helicopter's instrument panel, the display gives the crew a more concise view of the battlefield. They will have instant access to real time events. This includes the helicopter's flight path, manmade obstacles such as power lines, and even hostile threats "over the horizon."

Armor plating and an assortment of weapon systems offer protection to the crew. Just aft of the flight deck are two 7.62mm miniguns, and a .50-caliber machine gun is mounted at the rear of the helicopter on the exit ramp. While the mission of the Pave Low is primarily infiltration/exfiltration, it also serves as a helicopter gunship with its supply of weaponry.

MH-60 BLACKHAWK

The 160th SOAR(A) operates three Blackhawk variants. The MH-60K (Blackhawk) is a version of the Sikorsky UH-60 utility helicopter modified especially for special operations missions. These modifications include an extendable probe for aerial refueling (AR), sophisticated collection of aircraft survivability equipment (ASE), and improved navigation systems, allowing the helicopter to operate in the most austere environments and adverse weather conditions.

The MH-60K is a hybrid derivative of field-proven UH-60A Blackhawk. The helicopter is

powered by twin General Electric T700-GE-701C turboshaft engines rated at 1,700 hp each, an improved durability gearbox, and is aerial re-fuelable in a variety of tank configurations. It has a digital automatic flight control computer with coupled automatic approach/depart/hover functions. Other features include custom-designed airframe and landing gear for a high degree of battlefield survivability; hardened flight controls, with redundant electrical and hydraulic systems; a self-sealing, crash-resistant fuel system; and energy absorbing landing gear and crew seats. With fully integrated cockpit and avionics, it is capable of precise navigation, day or night, in all types weather conditions

The second variant is the MH-60L. Like the Pave Low, its primary mission is to carry out infil/exfil, along with re-supply operations in a variety of weather conditions.. Secondary missions of the MH-60 include external load, CSAR and MEDE-VAC operations. The MH-60 can operate from a fixed base, remote sites, or ship-borne operations.

Finally, the MH-60L direct action penetrator (DAP) is equipped with an assortment of weapons systems. The DAP has the primary mission of armed escort and fire support. It conducts close air support, employing precision-guided ordnance in the support

of infiltration or exfiltration of small units. The DAP can be called upon to perform any mission, day or night, in all types of adverse weather conditions.

MH-47 CHINOOK

The primary mission of the MH-47 is the overt and covert infiltration, exfiltration, air assault, and re-supply of SOF teams. The 160th SOAR (A) currently operates two models: the MH-47D adverse weather cockpit (AWC) which is capable of operating at night during the worst of weather conditions. With the use of special mission equipment and night vision devices, the aircrew can operate in hostile mission environments over all types of terrain, at low altitudes during periods of low visibility, and low ambient lighting conditions with pinpoint navigation. This is achieved by employing the aircraft's forward-looking infrared radar, and a navigation system consisting of a mission computer using GPS/INS/Doppler navigation.

The large cargo hold of the aircraft will easily fit an FAV/DPV. In addition to these vehicles, the hold can also fit an RSOV to provide the Rangers added support. The MH-47 is also fully capable of providing cover fire for any infl/exfil mission. The weapons array includes two M134 machine-guns and one M60D machine-gun located on the rear loading ramp.

The newest Chinook is the MH-47E, nicknamed the "Dark Horse." This heavy assault helicopter, like its sister ship, was specifically designed to support SOF missions. It has totally integrated avionics subsystems, combining backup avionics architecture with dual mission processors; remote

Left: A night vision image of a U.S. Army MH-47 Chinook helicopter pilot from the 3/160th Special Operations Aviation Regiment (SOAR) out of Hunter Army Airfield, Savannah, Georgia. The pilot is adjusting his AN/AVS-9 night vision goggles (NVG) prior to a night mission. *Defense Visual Information Center*

Below: The MH-60 direct action penetrator (DAP) is capable of mounting two M134 7.62mm miniguns, two 30mm chain-guns, two 19-shot 2.75 rocket pods, and Hellfire and Stinger missiles in a variety of combinations, depending on mission parameters. An integrated fire control system, combined with the pilot's head-up display (HUD) makes the DAP a precision weapons delivery platform, operational both day and night. The standard configuration of the DAP is one rocket pod, one 30mm cannon, and two miniguns. *USASOC*

terminal units; multifunction displays and display generators to improve combat survivability and mission reliability; an A/R probe for mid-air refueling; an external rescue hoist; and two L714 turbine engines. The aircraft's fuel tanks are integral, replacing the internal auxiliary fuel tanks usually carried on the MH-47D. The tanks provide 2,068 gallons of fuel with no loss of cargo space. Crew members for both MH-47 variants include a pilot, co-pilot, flight engineer, and two crew chiefs.

MH-6J LITTLE BIRD

The MH-6J, or Little Bird, is a single engine light utility helicopter based on the Hughes 500 Defender series. The MH-6J, currently manufactured by MD Helicopters, has been modified with outboard platforms on both sides of the aircraft. This configuration, known as the external personnel system, can accommodate a total of six external and two internal seating positions. The helicopter is capable of conducting covert infiltrations, exfiltrations, and combat assaults over varying terrain and in various weather conditions.

The small size and agility of the aircraft, combined with the capabilities of Night Stalker pilots, give these Little Birds the ability to navigate between buildings and skim along at street level. Should the war in Iraq turn into a MOUT environment, the Little Birds will prove indispensable for supporting SOF units.

In addition to its infil/exfil roles, it is also used for reconnaissance missions and for command and control. Its compact size allows for rapid deployment in C-130, C-141, C-17, and C-5 transport aircraft. Some aircraft are equipped with forward-looking infrared radar. The aircraft can be configured for fast roping operations, as well as special racks to insert and extract up to 2 motorcycles.

All crews are qualified to conduct NVG infil/exfil, short term airborne operations (STA-BOs), fast rope, and aerial suppression operations to urban, mountainous, desert, and jungle objectives, as well as to ships and offshore drilling platforms. Crews are trained in long-range precision navigation and formation flight over land and water to arrive at objectives at a prearranged time within 30 seconds. Maximum range with two auxiliary tanks installed is 400 nautical miles. Mission endurance with one auxiliary tank installed is 3 hours, 20 minutes, including a 20-minute reserve. The maximum endurance with 2 auxiliary tanks installed is 5 hours, including a 20 minute reserve.

AH-6J LIGHT ATTACK HELICOPTER

The AH-6J LAH is a highly modified version of the McDonnell Douglas 530 series commercial helicopter. The aircraft is a single turbine engine, dual flight control, light attack helicopter. It is primarily employed in close air support of ground troops, target destruction raids, and armed escort of other aircraft. A controllable, infrared surveillance system provides the pilots a TV video-type infrared image of terrain features and ground. The forward-looking infrared radar is a passive system and detects energy (long wavelength radiant IR) emitted, naturally or artificially, by any object in daylight or darkness. The helicopter can support a wide range of weaponry, ranging from 7.62mm mini-guns, to "Hellfire" antitank guided missiles.

CH-46 SEA KNIGHT

The CH-46E, or Sea Knight, is used by the U.S. Marine Corps to provide all-weather, day-or-night assault transport of combat troops, supplies and equipment. The Sea Knight's primary function is troop assault, while its secondary function is the movement of supplies and equipment. Additional tasks may be assigned, such as combat support, search and rescue, support for forward refueling and rearming points, medical evacuation, and

The AH-6J—"a Little Bird with an attitude"—provides CAS in support of the SOF operators. It can be fitted with a variety of weapons systems. The normal aircraft configuration consists of two 7.62mm miniguns with 1,500 to 2,000 rounds per gun, and two seven-shot 2.75-inch rocket pods. Alternate configurations include the M134 7.62mm minigun, a six-barrel, air-cooled, link-fed, electrically driven Gatling gun. The weapon has a rate of fire of 2,000 or 4,000 rpm, with a range of 100 to 750 meters. *USASOC*

recovery of aircraft and personnel. The Sea Knight has been in service since the Vietnam War, servicing the navy and marines with medium lift capability. The fleet of helicopters is scheduled to be replaced with the MH-60S Knight Hawk in 2004.

CH-53E SUPER STALLION

The CH-53E, or Super Stallion, is the Marine Corps' heavy lift helicopter, designed for the transportation of material and supplies. The helicopter is capable of lifting 16 tons, transporting the load 50 nautical miles, dropping it off, and returning. A typical load would be an M198 howitzer or a 26,000 pound light armored vehicle. The Super Stallion is equipped with a refueling probe and can be refueled in flight giving the helicopter indefinite range.

The CH-53E is a follow-on for its predecessor, the CH-53D. Improvements over the D model include the addition of a third engine to give the aircraft the ability to lift the majority of the Fleet Marine Force's equipment, a dual-point cargo hook system, improved main rotor blades, and composite tail rotor blades. A dual digital automatic flight control system and engine anti-ice system give the aircraft an all-weather capability.

The helicopter seats 37 passengers in its normal configuration and has provisions to carry 55 passengers with centerline seats installed. With the dual-point hook systems, it can carry external loads at increased airspeeds due to the stability achieved with the dual-point system. The CH-53E is compatible with most amphibious class ships and is carried routinely aboard such amphibious assault ship types as landing helicopter assault (LHA); landing platform helicopter (LPH); and landing helicopter dock (LHD. The CH-53 is slated for replacement by the MV-22 Osprey.

AH-1W COBRA

The AH-1W Super Cobra is the Marine Corps' day/night marginal weather attack helicopter provides escort for marine assault helicopters and their assault forces. The AH-1W has a crew of a pilot and gunner who sit in tandem. The twin-engine helicopter is capable of land- or sea-based operations. The AH-1W provides fire support and security for forward and rear area forces, point target/anti-armor, anti-helicopter, armed escort, supporting arms control and coordination, point and limited area air defense from enemy fixed-wing aircraft, and armed and visual reconnaissance.

The HH-60 is the U.S. Navy variation of the Blackhawk and is often used by the Navy SEALs as an insertion platform. Powered by two General Electric T700-GE-700 or T700-GE-701C engines with speeds of 180 knots and range of 380 nautical miles (600 km), it is normally armed with two 7.62mm machine guns mounted in the windows. Additional weapons systems include AGM-114 Hellfire or AGM-119 Penguin missiles, three MK46 or MK50 torpedoes, or additional .50-caliber machine guns mounted in the doors. It has a crew of three to four, depending on mission. *Defense Visual Information Center*

The AH-1W is operated in eight composite marine light attack helicopter squadrons composed of eighteen AH-1W Cobras and nine UH-1 "Hueys." The AH-1W is outfitted with a night yargeting system/forward-looking infrared radar that provides laser range-finding/designating and camera capabilities. The AH-1W is fully capable of performing its attack mission in all weather conditions. Whether moving across the open desert or operating in the close quarters of an urban envi-

ronment, the marines depend on Cobra helicopters to provide close-in fire support coordination in serial and ground escort operations.

AV-8B HARRIER II

While all other SOF ground force units must depend on air force or naval aircraft for close air support, the marines bring their support with them. Each amphibious ready group carries a compliment of six AV-8B Harriers. These unique "jump-jets" give the Leathernecks added punch for any assault and provide CAS for Force Recon teams on DA missions.

The AV-8B Harrier II is a vertical/short takeoff and landing (V/STOL) light-attack jet aircraft. This "jump jet" is a single-pilot aircraft with a primary mission to provide close air support for marine ground forces. The AV-8B is capable of operating from short fields, forward sites, roads, and surface ships providing minimum response time to targets. Though not as fast as other jet fighters, its unique vertical or short takeoffs, hovering, and vertical landing to deliver its ordnance from austere forward areas without the benefit of an air field.

OSPREY

The Osprey is a tilt-rotor vertical lift aircraft, which means it takes off like a helicopter and flies like a conventional airplane. However, there is nothing conventional about the Osprey. Development of the Osprey V-22 program began in 1981, originally for the U.S. Marines and designated the MV-22. The CV-22 will be a special operations variant of the MV-22. The mission of the CV-22 will be to infil/exfil and resupply special operations forces in

The CH-46 Sea Knight, lifting off from the USS *Saipan*, is the marines' medium lift assault helicopter. Powered by twin GE-T58-16 engines, it has a range of 132 nautical miles (151.8 miles) with a speed of 145 knots (166.75 miles per hour). The normal crew consists of a pilot, copilot, crew chief, and mechanic. For combat, the crew consists of a pilot, copilot, crew chief, and two aerial gunners. It is capable of transporting a maximum of 14 troops with aerial gunners, or 15 litters and two attendants. The CH-53E Super Stallion, in the background, is used for the transportation of heavy equipment and supplies. Three General Electric T64-GE-416 turboshaft engines give it a speed of 172 miles per hour with a range of 621 miles without refueling power it. It also has the capability to accommodate mid-air refueling, which increases its range indefinitely. It is armed with two XM218 .50-caliber machine guns. *US Navy*

The primary function of the AV-8B Harrier is to provide close air support for the marines. Its mission is to attack and destroy surface targets under day and night visual conditions. Manufactured by McDonnell Douglas and powered by a Rolls Royce F402-RR-406 or F402-RR-408 turbofan engine, it can provide CAS out to 163 nautical miles (187.45 miles) with a loiter time on station of 30 minutes. Moving at speeds from subsonic to transonic, it is armed with seven external store stations. These store stations are comprised of six wing stations for AIM-9 Sidewinder and an assortment of air-to-ground weapons, external fuel tanks, and AGM-65 Maverick missiles, and one centerline station for defense electronic countermeasures (DECM) pod or air-to-ground ordnance. A 25mm GAU-12, six-barrel gun pod can be mounted on the centerline and has a 300-round capacity with a lead computing optical sight system (LCOSS) gunsight. Here, the pilot is being directed through a pre-flight check prior to launch from the flight deck of the USS *Bataan*. US Navy

An AH-1W Super Cobra helicopter, assigned to the White Knights of Helicopter Squadron 165 (HMM-165) operating with the 13th MEU(SOC), is prepared to take off from the flight deck of the USS *Bonhomme Richard*. The AH-1W is primarily an attack helicopter, providing close in-air support and cover for marines on the ground. Powered by two General Electric T700-GE-401 engines, it can fly at a speed of 147 knots (169 miles per hour) with a range of 256 nautical miles (294.4 miles) in basic combat attack configuration. The crew consists of two officers, a pilot, and a gunner. Its armaments include one 20mm turreted cannon and four external wing stations. Its wing stations can fire 2.75-inch/5-inch rockets and a wide variety of precision guided missiles, including the TOW/Hellfire (point target/anti-armor), the Sidewinder (anti-air), and the Sidearm (anti-radar). *USMC*

denied or enemy area in total darkness and in all weather

The CV-22 will differ from the MV-22 in the addition of a third seat in the cockpit for a flight engineer, and will be fitted with a refueling probe to facilitate mid-air refueling. The AFSOC version of the Osprey will have the modern suite of electronics, like those installed in other AFSOC aircraft, including multi-mode terrain avoidance and terrain following radar.

It will have enhanced early warning equipment for increased battlefield awareness, with more than 2.5 times the volume of flares and chaff, radar jamming gear and improved integration of defensive countermeasures. For combat search and rescue it will have an internally mounted rescue hoist and a crew door located on the starboard side of the aircraft. Another significant difference between the CV-22 and the MV-22 will be the amount of fuel the CV-22 will carry, with approximately twice the amount of fuel of the marine variant.

CHAPTER SIX

INTELLIGENCE

The following are two ways the U.S. Department of Defense defines intelligence:

1. The product resulting from the collection, processing, integration, analysis, evaluation, and interpretation of available information concerning foreign countries or areas.

2. Information and knowledge about an adversary obtained through observation, investigation, analysis, or understanding.

It doesn't matter if operators have had the best training, or whether they are equipped with the latest weapons or technology. The one piece of the equation vital to success or failure is intelligence.

Intelligence can come from a variety of sources, ranging from reconnaissance satellites operating in a geo-synchronous orbit around the earth, an informant in a dark alley of some third world country. However, whether it is high tech or word of mouth, accurate information is paramount to any mission, in general, and especially critical in special operations missions.

Signals intelligence (SIGINT) is intelligence comprising either individually or in combination all communications intelligence, electronic intelligence, and foreign instrumentation signals intelligence, regardless of how it is transmitted. This includes, telephones, cell phones, satellite phones, radios, etc.

Human intelligence (HUMINT) is the collection of intelligence by human sources. Subsets of HUMINT include:

Counterintelligence (CI) involves activities which deal with identifying and counteracting the threat to security by Foreign Intelligence & Security Services (FISS) or by organizations and individuals engaged in espionage, sabotage, subversion, or terrorism; interrogation of prisoners of war (IPW); long-range surveillance (LRS); and human exploitation/ intelligence teams (HEITs).

When SOF units are assigned a mission, they have a number of intelligence-gathering agencies, both civilian and military, at their disposal. A vast array of information is gathered by the U.S. intelligence community over a dozen government agencies, such as the CIA, National Security Agency (NSA), and National Imagery and Mapping Agency (NIMA), along with an assortment of intelligence organizations from the armed forces providing information for various operations.

CIA

The CIA is an independent agency, responsible to the president through the Director of Central Intelligence. The mission of the CIA is to support the president, the National Security Council, and those individuals who make and execute U.S. national security policy by providing accurate, evidence-based, comprehensive, and timely foreign intelligence related to national security, and by conducting counterintelligence activities, special activities, and other functions related to foreign intelligence and national security, as directed by the president.

The CIA carries out research, development, and deployment of technology for intelligence activities. The agency functions as an autonomous source of analysis on subject matter of interest as well as interfacing with other organizations in the intelligence community, an interaction that has become more prevalent and necessary since the September 11 attacks. This alliance serves to ensure that the intelligence gathered and presented is the best intelligence possible, whether intended for the NCA or the theatre commander.

As America engages in the global war on terrorism, the CIA has addressed these new challenges by creating special centers to concentrate on high-priority issues such as nonproliferation of weapons of mass destruction, counterterrorism, counterintelligence, international organized crime and narcotics trafficking, environment, and arms control intelligence.

NATIONAL SECURITY AGENCY (NSA)

The NSA is a unified organization, which provides for the SIGINT mission of the U.S. and ensures secure communications systems for all departments and agencies of the U.S. government. Its operations are clandestine in nature, rating the highest level of security. For this reason, it is often referred to as the "No Such Agency." Its responsibilities are to function as the principal SIGINT authority to the Secretary of Defense, the Director of Central Intelligence, and the Joint Chiefs of Staff, keeping them fully informed on all SIGINT matters. The NSA transforms key SIGINT for use by the highest government and military decision-makers, monitoring, gathering, and decoding foreign communications (signals) from around the world, as well as performing information assurance, protecting both U.S. security and communications from exploitation.

National Reconnaissance Office (NRO)

The National Reconnaissance Office provides the U.S. its eyes and ears in space. The NRO's mission is to enable U.S. global information superiority, during peace through war. The NRO ensures the technology and spaceborne assets (i.e., satellites) needed to acquire timely intelligence worldwide are always available to the NCA and the military. These satellites provide an objective, reliable, and responsive source of information with near real-time information support for a wide range of objectives.

Operating as a separate agency of the Department of Defense, the NRO is managed jointly by the Secretary of Defense and the Director of Central Intelligence. The Director of Central Intelligence establishes the organization's collection priorities and requirements. The NRO is responsible for the distinctive and innovative technology, large-scale systems, engineering, development and acquisition, and operation of space reconnaissance systems and related intelligence activities needed to support global information superiority.

From its satellites orbiting miles above the Earth, NRO provides America's national and military leaders with data warning of potential military aggression, monitors weapons of mass destruction programs, tracks terrorists, enforces arms control and environmental treaties, and assesses the impact of natural and manmade disasters.

National Imagery and Mapping Agency (NIMA)

National Imagery and Mapping Agency is a Department of Defense combat support agency, thereby a member of the intelligence community and is the principal provider of geospatial intelligence information supporting NCA and the military. NIMA provides timely, relevant, and accurate geospatial intelligence in support of national security. NIMA is the central repository for imagery and mapping, created to exploit the tremendous potential of enhanced collection systems, digital processing technology, and the prospective expansion of commercial imagery.

NIMA's imagery and intelligence also supports national decision-making processes, contributing to the high state of operational readiness of America's military forces. The agency's geospatial intelligence comes in all forms, from a variety of sources (e.g., imagery, imagery intelligence, and geospatial data and information).

NIMA defines geospatial intelligence as "the exploitation and analysis of cartographic, imagery and geodetic information to describe, assess, and visually depict physical features and geographically referenced activities on the Earth."

Shuttle Radar Topography Mission (SRTM)

The Shuttle Radar Topography Mission was a joint project of NIMA and the National Aeronautics and Space Administration (NASA). The SRTM used a specially customized radar system to capture the elevation data, synthetic aperture radar and single-pass radar interferometry. Two radar images were captured simultaneously, one from the radar antenna on board the Space Shuttle Endeavour's payload bay, and the other from an antenna at the end of a 200-foot mast. The objective of this project was to create digital topographic data of the Earth's land surface. The elevation data's absolute vertical accuracy is to within 16 meters. This radar system collected data

The U2 spy plane was first deployed in 1955 with the primary mission of high-altitude reconnaissance, monitoring Soviet activities during the Cold War. It is powered by one General Electric F-118-101 engine with a range of 7,000 miles and a ceiling of 70,000 feet. *Defense Visual Information Center*

that will result in the first-ever, most complete, high-resolution database of the Earth's topography. SRTM may prove to be one of the best geospatial collection tools in the history of mapping.

TERRAIN VISUALIZATION

The National Imagery and Mapping Agency creates highly accurate terrain visualization maneuvering support through the integration of its orthorectified imagery and digital terrain elevation data. Using these standard NIMA products, the agency's software architecture can create, in real-time, highly accurate, geo-specific scenes for viewing on a workstation's computer screen monitor. Digital maps can be synchronized to the imagery for reference positions. This three-dimensional terrain visualization has become a valuable tool used by national and military decision makers for mission planning and rehearsals. When used in conjunction with artificial intelligence, SOF units can actually run through a simulated adaptation of the mission. Teams can determine the best route through the mountains, location of the target building, and other factors before they ever leave their base.

INTELLIGENCE AIRCRAFT

In addition to the intelligence community's satellites, there are a number of aircraft used to perform intelligence-gathering missions. The limitations of the satellites are that they do not "camp" in one spot, but only pass over areas as they orbit the Earth. Additionally, they are limited by high altitude, cloud cover, and other atmospheric conditions. For this reason, specialty aircraft have been designed for intelligence gathering.

The history of high-tech intelligence aircraft goes back to the legendary U-2 which flew missions over Cuba, Russia and other communist countries during the Cold War. Today's aircraft includes the state of the art unmanned aerial vehicles (UAVs)

Joint surveillance and target attack radar systems (JSTARS) bring airborne battle management to a new level of sophistication. With a flight crew of four plus 15 Air Force and three Army specialists, the aircraft has a range of nine hours. Orbiting at a ceiling of 42,000 feet at 390 to 510 knots, the E-8C provides intelligence to combatant commanders to maintain control of the battle-space and conduct action against enemy forces. The aircraft delivers real time information necessary to enhance ground situation awareness by means of intelligence support, attack support, and targeting operations, including attack aviation, naval surface fire, field artillery, and friendly maneuver forces. *Defense Visual Information Center Graphic*

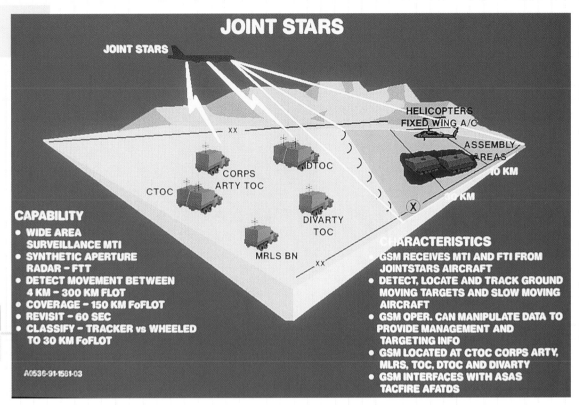

JOINT STARS

JOINT STARS

HELICOPTERS
FIXED WING A/C

ASSEMBLY AREAS

10 KM

CORPS
ARTY TOC

DTOC

CTOC

DIVARTY
TOC

MRLS BN

CAPABILITY
- WIDE AREA SURVEILLANCE MTI
- SYNTHETIC APERTURE RADAR – FTT
- DETECT MOVEMENT BETWEEN 4 KM – 300 KM FLOT
- COVERAGE – 150 KM FoFLOT
- REVISIT – 60 SEC
- CLASSIFY – TRACKER vs WHEELED TO 30 KM FoFLOT

CHARACTERISTICS
- GSM RECEIVES MTI AND FTI FROM JOINTSTARS AIRCRAFT
- DETECT, LOCATE AND TRACK GROUND MOVING TARGETS AND SLOW MOVING AIRCRAFT
- GSM OPER. CAN MANIPULATE DATA TO PROVIDE MANAGEMENT AND TARGETING INFO
- GSM LOCATED AT CTOC CORPS ARTY, MLRS, TOC, DTOC AND DIVARTY
- GSM INTERFACES WITH ASAS TACFIRE AFATDS

A0536-91-1581-03

This graphic explains the JSTARS battlefield surveillance system. The radar and computer subsystems on the E-8C gather and display general and specific data concerning the battlefield environment. As events unfold, it collects tracking information on enemy and friendly ground forces. This information is transmitted in near-real time to the Army's common ground stations, via a secure jam-resistant control data link, and to additional ground command, control, communications, computers, and intelligence (C4I) nodes beyond line-of-sight (LOS), via ultra high frequency satellite communications. *Defense Visual Information Center Graphic*

such as the Predator and Global Hawk, which can loiter over battlefields or intelligence targets for hours feeding back real-time information. This information can then be evaluated and used as a basis to formulate SOF missions. Additionally, the UAV has crossed over from being just a data-gathering asset, to an aircraft cable of engaging the enemy on the spot, making it the first unmanned combat aerial vehicle (UCAV) to enter actual combat.

U-2

Since the early days of the Cold War, when these planes would fly over the Soviet Union, Cuba, and other Communist nations, the mission of the U-2 has been to provide continuous day and night, high-altitude, all-weather surveillance and reconnaissance in direct support of U.S. and allied ground and air forces. The data obtained by these missions provided crucial intelligence to U.S. decision makers.

The U-2 is a single-seat, single-engine, high-altitude, surveillance and reconnaissance aircraft.

The U-2 has a glider-like appearance with its long, narrow, straight wings. These features allow the aircraft to carry the heavy sensor payloads to unparalleled altitudes rapidly, and remain at high altitude for an extended period. The U-2 is capable of collecting multi-sensor photo, electro-optic, infrared, and radar imagery, as well as signals intelligence data. It can downlink all data, except photo imagery, in near real time, to anywhere in the world, providing the NCA, theatre commanders, and operators with the latest possible intelligence.

Other key E-8C missions equipment includes communications, operations, and control subsystems. During a mission, 18 workstations present computer-processed information in graphic as well as tabular format on a video display. The operators and technicians carry out battle management, surveillance, weapons, intelligence, communications, and maintenance functions. *Defense Visual Information Center*

E-8C JSTARS

The E-8C joint surveillance target attack radar system (Joint STARS) is an airborne battle management and command and control (C2) aircraft. The mission of the JSTARS is performing ground surveillance to form an assessment of the enemy's position and strength, and to support attack operations, targeting the enemy. The E-8C provides dedicated support of ground and air theatre commanders.

The E-8C is built on a commercial Boeing 707-300 series airframe, significantly remanufactured and modified with the radar, communications, operations, and control subsystems required to perform its mission. The most prominent external feature is its 40-foot long, canoe-shaped

Defense Visual Information Center Photo A high-angle view of a P-3C Orion in flight over thick cloud cover. Although the Orion's primary mission is maritime and anti-submarine operations, it is equally at home over terra firma, providing commanders and ground forces alike with intelligence and recognizance in a battlefield environment. *Defense Visual Information Center*

radome under the forward fuselage. This radome houses the 24-foot long, side-looking phased array antenna. The antenna can be tilted to either side of the aircraft where it can develop a 120-degree field of view covering nearly 19,305 square miles, and is capable of detecting targets at more than 156 miles. The radar operates in several modes including wide-area surveillance, moving target indicator (MTI), fixed target indicator (FTI) target classification, and synthetic aperture radar.

The E-8C can fly a mission profile for 9 hours without refueling. Its range and on-station time can be substantially increased through in-flight refueling. The E-8C can respond rapidly to support military contingency operations worldwide. The aircraft is equipped with a jam-resistant system capable of operating while encountering intense electronic countermeasures.

RC-135V/W RIVET JOINT

The RC-135V/W Rivet Joint reconnaissance aircraft supports NCA and theatre commanders with near real-time, on-scene intelligence collection, analysis and distribution capabilities.

The Rivet Joint is a highly modified C-135. These modifications encompass the aircraft's onboard sensor suite, which allows the mission crew to detect, identify, and geolocate signals throughout the electromagnetic spectrum. The crew forwards the gathered data in a variety of formats via Rivet Joint's sizable communications suite. The aircraft can accommodate up to thirty-two people, including the

An RC-135W rivet joint reconnaissance aircraft of the Air Combat command flies a training mission. The RC-135 works closely with the E-3A aircraft airborne warning and control system (AWACS), providing direct, near real-time reconnaissance information and electronic warfare support to theater combatant commanders and combat forces. It has three pilots and two navigators, with a flight crew numbering from 21 to 27, depending on mission requirements. *Defense Visual Information Center*

cockpit crew, electronic warfare officers, intelligence operators, and in-flight maintenance technicians.

P3-C ORION

The P-3C is a four-engine turboprop, land-based, long-range, anti-submarine warfare (ASW), and maritime surveillance aircraft. Primarily designed as an ASW patrol aircraft, the Orion is equipped with an avionics system integrated by a general-purpose digital computer. This combination supports all tactical displays and monitors, automatically launches ordnance, and provides flight information to the pilots. The systems of this airborne information coordinates navigation information and accepts sensor data inputs for tactical display and storage.

The Orion aircraft has served U.S. ground forces in the search for terrorists in Afghanistan, and will be more than capable of providing the same intelligence as U.S. forces head toward Baghdad.

RQ-1 PREDATOR UAV

The RQ-1 Predator is an unmanned aerial vehicle, or UAV. It is a joint forces air asset used to provide medium-altitude, long-endurance reconnaissance,

This photo shows the vast amount of intelligence gathering systems packed into the Rivet Joint reconnaissance aircraft. The navigator checks one of the myriad of systems vital to the plane's mission. If the aircraft is out of position by even 1/100th of a mile, it would have a critical effect on battlefield data. *Defense Visual Information Center*

Members of the 11th Reconnaissance Squadron at Indian Springs, Nevada, perform a pre-flight check on a RQ-1L Predator unmanned aerial vehicle (UAV) prior to a mission. In support of the global war on terrorism, the squadron has been deployed to a classified location. The primary mission of the Predator is airborne surveillance reconnaissance and target acquisition. Powered by a Rotax 914 four-cylinder engine, it has a cruising speed of 84 miles per hour with a range of 400 nautical miles. It can fly up to a ceiling of 25,000 feet and can loiter in an area for 24 hours. *Defense Visual Information Center*

surveillance, and target acquisition in support of the Joint Force theatre commander.

The RQ-1A/B Predator is not merely an unmanned aircraft; it is a complete system. The organization of the operational system includes: four UAVs equipped with sensors, a ground control station (GCS), and a Predator Primary Satellite Link (PPSL). It is manned with fifty-five personnel, providing for continuous 24-hour operation. It can operate both in the day and night, transmitting real-time video to ground forces with enough resolution to clearly see an individual's facial features. The Predator B has an operational ceiling of 45,000 feet, and a maximum payload of 750 pounds. It is capable of carrying up to fourteen Hellfire II anti-armor missiles.

The standard crew for the Predator consists of a pilot and two sensor operators. The team will operate the UAV from inside the GCS via a C-Band line-of-sight (LOS) data link or a Ku-Band satellite data link for beyond line-of-sight flight. The Predator is outfitted with a color nose camera, which is generally used by the aerial vehicle operator for flight control, a day variable aperture TV camera, a variable aperture infrared camera (for low light/night), and a synthetic aperture radar (SAR) for looking through smoke, clouds, or haze. The cameras produce full motion video and SAR still-frame radar images. The three sensors are carried on the same airframe but cannot be operated simultaneously.

AGM-114 Hellfire

The Hellfire Air-to-Ground Missile System (AGMS) provides heavy anti-armor capability. The

Taking the UAV to the next level, the CIA put forward a new theory. The idea was that by the time information is relayed to the appropriate force, it may be too late to carry out an accurate or significant attack against the enemy. In lieu of this challenge, the CIA developed the concept of fitting the Predator with Hellfire missiles and a laser designator to guide the projectiles to their target. This concept became reality in the skies over Yemen last November. A Predator armed with two Hellfire missiles acquired, tracked, launched, and destroyed a vehicle transporting senior members of Al Qaeda. In that moment, the UAV became an unmanned combat aerial vehicle (UCAV). *USAF*

The Predator carries electro-optical, infrared cameras, and synthetic aperture radar (SAR). The SAR permits the UAV to "see" through heavy cloud cover, providing a clear picture of the battlefield below. The two-color daylight television (DLTV) is fitted with variable zoom and 955mm lenses. The high resolution forward-looking infrared (FLIR) has six fields of view ranging from 19 to 560mm. The RQ-1 is fitted with a multispectral targeting systems (MTS), which provide real-time imagery selectable between infrared and DLTV and laser designation capability.

18-pound AGM-114 missile warhead incorporates a conical "shaped charge" with a copper liner cone, forming a jet of molten metal that penetrates the armor. Although the actual penetration data is classified, this high explosive (HE) antitank warhead is effective against a variety of armor, including reactive and appliqué. In addition to armored vehicles, the Hellfire can also be used against concrete bunkers and comparable fortifications.

The missile is propelled by a single stage, single thrust, and solid propellant motor. When the thrust exceeds 500 to 600 pounds, the AGM-114 leaves the rail, with a maximum velocity of 950 miles per hour. Arming of the missile takes place between 150 to 300 meters after launch. It has a speed of Mach 1.3, with a range of 8,000 meters.

GLOBAL HAWK

The Global Hawk Unmanned Aerial Vehicle provides theatre commanders with near real-time and high-resolution intelligence, surveillance, and reconnaissance imagery via satellite and ground systems. Operating at exceptionally high altitudes, the Global Hawk can survey substantial geographic areas with pinpoint accuracy.

From UAV to UCAV

On November 3, 2002, the Predator UAV went from a reconnaissance platform to America's first unmanned combat aerial vehicle (UCAV). After tracking six suspected Al Qaeda terrorists for weeks, members of the CIA's Special Activities division performed an air strike on their vehicle 100 miles east of the Yemeni capital of San'a using a Predator equipped with AGM-114 Hellfire missiles. Afterward, all that remained was dust and debris.

One of the terrorists was later identified as Qaed Senyan al-Harthi (a.k.a. Abu Ali), considered Al Qaeda's top man in Yemen and believed to have been involved in the October 2000 attack on the USS Cole, resulting in the deaths of seventeen U.S. sailors.

Defense Secretary Donald Rumsfeld commented on the report of al-Harthi's death: "It would be a very good thing if he were out of business."

The AGM-114 Hellfire II missile is shown here mounted to the wing of an AH-64 Apache gunship. The RQ-1, preparing for battle in Iraq, is capable of carrying up to fourteen Hellfire II anti-armor missiles. The Hellfire has a speed of 1.3 mach and carries an 18-pound charge in its warhead. It has a range of 8,000 meters.

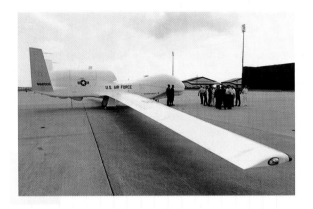

The RQ-4A Global Hawk is a high altitude, long-range and long endurance UAV that performs many of the same missions as the U-2. It is often considered a complement to the U-2, and there is some discussion whether it could replace the aging Cold War spy plane. The Global Hawk has double the range, three times the loiter cycle, and, most significantly, does not depend on a pilot. Its mission is airborne intelligence, surveillance, and reconnaissance (ISR). *Defense Visual Information Center*

Baghdad, Iraq's capital city, is located in a broad plain, with a population of nearly 4 million. The Tigris River is visible beginning at the upper left of the image (north). Canals are discernible throughout the city. The runways of the Baghdad International Airport are visible midway between the center and the bottom of the image (west of the city center). Even after the 1991 Gulf War, Baghdad remained the major commercial and industrial center of the country. *NASA*

Here is bomb damage assessment (BDA) intelligence imagery of Baath Party Headquarters in Baghdad. *Defense Visual Information Center*

This information provides the military with the most up-to-date data concerning enemy resources, location, and personnel.

Once the mission parameters are programmed into Global Hawk, the UAV can operate autonomously. This means it will taxi, take off, fly, and remain on station, capturing imagery, then return and land without any human intervention. Ground-based operators monitor UAV status and are able to change navigation and sensor plans during flight.

Global Hawks are equipped with electro-optical, infrared, and synthetic aperture radar sensors. This UAV is powered by one AE 3007 Turbofan, enabling the aircraft to reach speeds of 400 miles per hour. The main fuselage is aluminum, with over half the remaining components—including the wings, engine cover, engine intake, three radomes, and other components—made of lightweight, high-strength composite materials. *USAF*

Global Hawk has a wingspan of 116 feet and is 44 feet long, and can fly at speeds approaching 400 miles per hour. It has a range of 12,000 nautical miles, reaching altitudes of up to 65,000 feet, for durations up to 35 hours. A typical mission will see the aircraft fly 1,200 miles to an area of interest and remain on station for 24 hours. Its cloud-penetrating synthetic aperture radar/ground moving target indicator, electro-optical and infrared sensors can image an area the size of Illinois—40,000 nautical square miles—in just 24 hours.

CHAPTER SEVEN

WAR ON TERRORISM

SOCOM WORLD TOUR

In the global war on terrorism, U.S. Special Operations' "operational tempo," or pace of operations, is higher than ever before. These elite warriors will seek out the enemies of freedom and liberty in the "Axis of Evil" and beyond, in Afghanistan, Iraq, the Korean peninsula, the Philippines, and even the island of Bali. As President George W. Bush said, "They will bring them to justice, or bring justice to them."

OPERATION ENDURING FREEDOM

On October 19, 2001, four MC-130 Combat Talons from the Air Force Special Operations Command delivered 199 Rangers from the 3rd Battalion, 75th Ranger Regiment to Objective Rhino, located southwest of Kandahar, Afghanistan. The Ranger assault force was supported by AC-130 Spectre gunships as they seized a desert landing strip, engaged Taliban combatants, and secured the area as a forward aerial refuel/rearm point for future operations. Members of the AFSOC Special Tactics Team were embedded into the task force and provided vital information on the desert landing site to accommodate aircraft for follow-on forces. This site, later dubbed Camp Rhino, became the jumping off point for the U.S. Marines in Afghanistan.

Prior to the Ranger assault on Objective Rhino, and before the Marines could establish their base camp, Navy SEALs conducted special reconnaissance on suspected Al Qaeda and Taliban forces throughout the region. Though SEALs are often referred to as waterborne commandos, the "L" in their name means they are equally capable for operations on terra firma.

Members of the 3rd Battalion, 75th Ranger Regiment load onto an MC-130 Combat Talon. These Rangers would eventually parachute into Objective Rhino, located southwest of Kandahar, Afghanistan. Their mission was to seize and secure an airstrip for use as a forward arming and resupply point (FARP). *DoD*

SEAL teams performed a wide variety of missions, including sensitive site exploitation and search and destroy missions. The platoons would find themselves in caves, houses, compounds, and underground complexes. Such responsibilities netted the SEALs tons of ammunition, weapons, and intelligence material on terrorist forces.

SOF WITH NORTHERN ALLIANCE

Afghanistan's mountainous terrain made traveling by conventional methods difficult, and far from stealthy. For this reason, SOF teams employed a more local means of transportation—the horse. One special forces soldier even contacted headquarters to locate an old manual on cavalry operations. SOCOM is used to getting unique requests from its operators in the field, but few quite as unusual as a request for saddles.

In direct action missions, special forces soldiers coordinated air attacks using state-of-the-art tech-

nology to help neutralize Taliban forces, and directed the Northern Alliance success at Mazar-e-Sharif. Members of the Northern Alliance were encouraged to look through their SOFLAM and night vision goggles to target enemy positions. The SOF allies found these high-tech gadgets fascinating.

In a Pentagon briefing, Secretary of Defense Donald Rumsfeld put it this way: "U.S. special operations forces are on the ground in southern Afghanistan. They are not acting with tribes or factions, but are contributing in their own ways."

Deputy Secretary of Defense Paul Wolfowitz at a press conference in Washington related the following account of special forces actions in Operation Enduring Freedom (from a situation report of a special forces soldier dated October 25, 2001):

I am advising a man on how to best employ light infantry and horse cavalry in the attack against Taliban T-55s, mortars, artillery, personnel carriers and machine guns—a tactic which I think became outdated with the invention of the Gatling gun. The Mujahadeen have done that every day we have been on the ground. They

High-tech meets old world as Master Sergeant Bart Decker, an Air Force combat controller, rides horseback with the Northern Alliance in Afghanistan. Before entering the country, Decker provided air traffic control support for the initial airflow supporting Operation Enduring Freedom. It was not uncommon to see special operations forces swapping the vehicles for horses in the mountainous terrain of Afghanistan. Using horses, cell phones, SOFLAMs, and SatCom, these elite forces brought in precision fire on the Taliban and Al Qaeda forces. The operators' willingness to use animal transportation served as a bond between the forces and the locals. *DoD*

have attacked with 10 rounds of AK-47 ammunition per man, with snipers having less than 100 rounds . . . little water and less food.

We have witnessed the horse cavalry bounding overwatch from spur to spur to attack Taliban strong points—the last several kilometers under mortar, artillery and sniper fire. There is little medical care if injured, only a donkey ride to the aid station, which is a dirt hut. I think the Mujahadeen are doing very

well with what they have. They have killed over 125 Taliban . . . while losing only eight.

We couldn't do what we are doing without the close air support. Everywhere I go the civilians and Mujahadeen soldiers are always telling me they are glad the U.S.A. has come. They all speak of their hopes for a better Afghanistan once the Taliban are gone. Better go. My local commander is finishing his phone call with someone back in the U.S.

Departed position from which I spoke to you last night (November 9). We left on horse and linked up with the remainder of the element. I had a meeting with commander. We then departed from our initial linkup location and rode on begged, borrowed, and confiscated transportation. While it looked like a ragtag procession, the morale into Mazar-e-Sharif was triumphant. The locals loudly greeted us and thanked all Americans. Much waving, cheering, and clapping, even from the women. The U.S. Navy and Air Force did a great job. I am very proud of my men who have performed exceptionally well under very extreme conditions. I have personally witnessed heroism under fire by two U.S. non-commissioned officers, one army, one air force, when we came under direct artillery fire last night, which was less than 50 meters from me. When I ordered them to call close air support, they did so immediately without flinching even though they were under fire. As you know, a U.S. element was nearly overrun four days ago and continued to call close air support and ensured the Mujahadeen forces did not suffer a defeat. These two examples are typical of the performance of your soldiers and airmen. Truly uncommon valor has been a common virtue.

Afghan National Army

Teaching multi-ethnic Afghan recruits soldiering skills may be a new development in the global war against terrorism, but for the U.S. Green Berets of 1st Battalion, 3rd Special Forces Group (Airborne), it's a core mission they have mastered.

The Afghanistan National Army's first regular army battalion underwent 10 weeks of basic infantry and combat skills training at the Afghan Military

Members of the Navy SEAL teams provided valuable information by conducting special reconnaissance for fellow SOF units. They were instrumental in performing sensitive site exploitation (SSE) missions.

Academy in Kabul. New recruits in the Afghan National Army received training, advising and assistance from U.S. Army Special Forces members.

U.S. Special Forces members, assigned to 1st Battalion, 3rd Special Forces Group stationed at Fort Bragg, N.C., were tasked with providing the training for several battalions before commissioned and non-commissioned Afghan officers could assume responsibility for training future Afghan soldiers. U.S. Green Berets were faced with the daunting challenge of developing the nucleus of a national army with recruits representing all provinces within Afghanistan.

Classes taught by U.S. Army Special Forces included basic rifle marksmanship, weapons maintenance class and drill and ceremony training. As part of the training, recruits took part in a competitive drill conducted by U.S. Special Forces members at an Academy firing range. Several squads of Afghan recruits competed against one another in marksmanship and obstacle course races.

The training was in line with long-term U.S. and United Nations plans for providing Afghanistan's

Inserted early in the war, special forces ODAs worked closely with the Northern Alliance to conduct military operations against Taliban and Al Qaeda forces. Here, special forces soldiers provide cover, while a member of the Northern Alliance communicates via CB radio. The Northern Alliance forces would utilize CB radios to communicate with their Taliban adversaries, discussing terms of surrender but also taunting them as well. *DoD*

Special forces team "Tiger 03" sights in on an enemy force with a SOFLAM. The team will provide pinpoint accuracy for the delivery of a 2,000-pound smart bomb. The coordinated effort of SF and AFSOC combat controllers on the ground with U.S. aircraft overhead proved to be a lethal combination in Operation Enduring Freedom. *DoD*

internal and external security through a national army and police force. The forming and training of a national army is one of the cornerstones for a successful Afghan government. The training program calls for U.S. forces to train up to 18 battalions of infantry soldiers as the future core of the Afghan National Army. Some Afghan military leaders desire the formation of a 200,000-man army, provided they can get the financing.

From the initial insertion into the mountainous terrain, to the complex cave systems of Tora Bora, to the battle of Mazar-e-Sharif, to hunting down Taliban and Al Qaeda forces in Operation Anaconda in the mountains of Shah-e-Kot, U.S. Special Operations forces have demonstrated their mastery of the Art of War in Afghanistan. This is perhaps best summarized by the comments of General Charles R. Holland, commander, U.S. Special Operations Command during a visit to soldiers of the 5th Special Forces Group in Mazar-E-Sharif in December 2001: "Your actions have redefined the meaning of unconventional warfare."

In addition to the SOF units operating in Afghanistan, members of the U.S Army Special Forces and Delta Force teams were active in the Philippines, performing foreign internal defense missions, conducting company-level training with field companies of the Philippine Army, and hunting down Al Qaeda cells. At the same time, approximately 800 U.S. Special Forces soldiers have been operating out of Djibouti in the Horn of Africa. This location places these commandos within striking distance of terrorist cells operating in both Yemen and Somalia.

Operation Iraqi Freedom

President Bush stated in December of 2002: "Saddam Hussein will fully disarm himself of weapons of

A Force Reconnaissance marine and a member of the security element prepare to move out in one of the many towns in Afghanistan. *USMC*

Tech. Sgt. Mike Buytas Soldiers from 1st Battalion, 3rd Special Forces Group stationed at Fort Bragg, North Carolina, were tasked with providing the training for several battalions before commissioned and noncommissioned Afghan officers can assume responsibility for training future Afghan soldiers. Here, an SF soldier trains a member of the Afghan army in marksmanship. *USAF*

mass destruction. And if he does not, the United States will lead a coalition to disarm him." Speaking at Fort Hood, Texas, January 2003, President Bush demonstrated his resolve in his comments on the fate of the Iraqi regime: "(T)hey may choose the path of peace or the path of war, and if force becomes necessary America will attack. America will attack, not to conquer, but for the advancement of peace."

Conventional forces were engaged in a high percentage of the missions to depose Saddam. From the tanks and infantry, to the fighters and stealth bombers, each worked in concert to bring a formidable force to bear on this repressive, vicious dictator. These forces stood ready throughout the region for the eventual attack into Iraq. However, before the first bullet was fired, the operators of the U.S.

Special forces members load onto a MH-47 helicopter in the Philippines. These ODAs, along with other special operations forces, were in the area performing FID missions, conducting company-level training with field companies of the Philippine army, and hunting down Al Qaeda cells. Crew members from the 160th Special Operations Aviations Regiment (Airborne) stand ready with M4s in hand, while the soldiers load the aircraft. *DoD*

The Rescue of Private Jessica Lynch

One of the most high-profile special operations mission conducted during Operation Iraqi Freedom was the rescue of Private First Class Jessica Lynch. On March 23, 2003, Iraqi forces, dressed in civilian clothing, ambushed an American convoy. Lynch, assigned to the 507th Ordnance Maintenance Company, based out of Fort Bliss, Texas, was among those soldiers attacked. CENTCOM reports indicated that the convoy had taken a wrong turn near the area of Nasiriyah and it was assaulted by Iraqi soldiers.

How many of the Americans survived the attack was not reported by CENTCOM, nor was information regarding what sort of resistance these support troops gave their attackers. An account of the attack by *The Washington Post* did state, however, that Lynch engaged the enemy until her ammunition ran out. She eventually became their prisoner of war and was held in the confines of the Saddam Hospital. At the time, the hospital was being utilized by the Iraqi regime as a command center in Nasiriyah. The compound was not unfamiliar to CENTCOM, as suspicions had surfaced that Ali Hassan al Majeed, known as "Chemical Ali" because he ordered the gassing of Kurdish villages in 1988, was operating out of the same facility.

When an Iraqi citizen whose wife was a nurse working in the hospital came to visit her, he noticed that the security of facility was increased. When he inquired to the reason behind this, he was informed that there was an American soldier being held at the hospital. The man, who would become know simply as Mohammed, sought out this wounded prisoner. He even managed to get into the room where Lynch was staying and was able to speak with her.

There, he observed the Iraqis beating her and treating her cruelly. It was then that this courageous individual made up his mind: He had to get help for this young woman. Upon leaving the compound, he traveled for five days, until he made contact with a unit of U.S. Marines. He related the information regarding the America soldier and where she was being held. Though apprehensive at first, the Marines eventually believed the man, and the information was conveyed up the chain of command.

Acting on this intelligence, U.S. special operations forces went into action and developed a rescue plan to extract

Lynch from her captors. Mohammed would be pressed into service for the rescue as he returned to the hospital twice, verifying that Jessica was still there and noting where her room was located. He also drew five detailed maps of the hospital and relayed the number of guards (41), their positions, and weapons.

On the night of April 1, the Marines began an assault in An Nasiriya, which was a diversion to draw attention away from the hospital. According to CENT-COM reports, the operation consisted of Army Rangers, Air Force pilots and combat controllers, U.S. Marines, and Navy SEALs. "It was a classic joint operation done by some of our nation's finest warriors, who are dedicated to never leaving a comrade behind," the report added.

Overhead reconnaissance aircraft monitored the surrounding area as the rescue unfolded below. With the Marines pressing their diversionary attacks, special operations forces units landed outside the hospital. Members of the 75th Ranger Regiment provided security while the rescue element, armed with suppressed M4A1 carbines, entered the facility in search of the fellow American. As the team entered into a room on the first floor of the hospital, the commandoes called out to her, "Jessica Lynch, we're United States soldiers and we're here to protect you and to take you home." When a commando approached the bed where Lynch was, she looked up at her rescuer and said, "I'm an American soldier, too."

The team's doctor quickly examined her whereupon she was strapped onto a stretcher and carried down a stairway and out to a waiting MH-60 Blackhawk helicopter. The operation from start to finish to took only 25 minutes, shaving a full 20 minutes off the 45 minute time that had been estimated. In addition to the rescue of the young woman, the special operations forces' operators located and recovered 11 bodies of those soldiers who had been killed when the convoy was first attacked. When completed, Lynch's rescue would be the first successful one of an American POW from enemy territory since World War II. After being rescued, Lynch was sent to Landstuhl Regional Medical Center in Germany so that she could fully recover from her injuries.

Special Operations forces will have already been on the scene.

In a Pentagon news briefing on April 1, 2003, Rumsfeld made the following comparison between Operation Desert Storm and Operation Iraqi Freedom:

[The Gulf War] was a sustained 38-day air campaign, followed by a brief ground attack. Instead, in this case, the ground attack actually started before the air war, with thousands of special forces pouring into all regions of the country and a large force rolling across the Kuwait border into southern Iraq.

In northern Iraq, special forces ODAs operated with the Patriotic Union of Kurdistan Forces in the weeks prior to Operation Iraqi Freedom to prepare

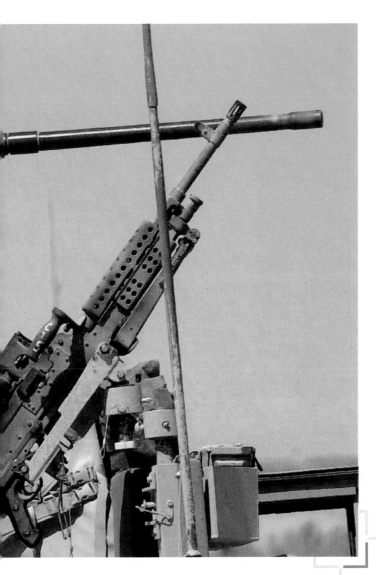

650 "Taliban-like" forces funded by both Saddam Hussein and Al Qaeda. The cities of Mosul, Kirkuk, and Tikrit were all captured at the hands of the Kurdish guerillas in coordination with U.S. Special Forces.

At the time, Brigadier General Vincent Brooks, deputy director of operations for CENTCOM, elaborated on the effort: "Our coalition special operations forces maintain pressure on the Iraqi military forces in northern Iraq through precision air strikes directed against the regular army fifth corps. Our searches in the Ansar al-Islam training camp continue, with coalition and Kurdish peshmerga working closely together."

U.S. Army Rangers from the 75th Ranger Regiment, supported by the paratroopers of the 173rd Airborne Brigade, performed a low-level parachute drop using C-17 Globemaster transport aircraft. These forces secured the airfield in Bashur, Northern Iraq. AFSOC assets provided air traffic control for the Rangers. This airborne assault was heralded as the most intricate combat airborne operation since World War II. A makeshift sign later identified the airfield as "Bush International Airport."

The Rangers also performed airfield seizure of two major airfields, H-2 and H-3, in western and southwestern Iraq. In addition to seizing the airfields, the Rangers also assaulted the Baath Party Headquarters in western Iraq, and attacked command and control sites throughout the country, cutting off the communications network between the regime and its forces.

Members of the 75th Ranger Regiment were instrumental in seizing the Hadithah dam and protecting it from destruction at the hands of the Iraqi

them for battle against Iraqi army units. In the early days of the operation, these forces captured a region occupied by Islamic extremist group Ansar al-Islam in northern Iraq. From atop their mountain perch, special forces soldiers employed .50 Barrett sniper rifles to engage the enemy positions. Over 1,000 Kurdish fighters and approximately 100 SOF operators took part in the assault, rousting an estimated

Members of the 75th Ranger Regiment seen here are in an operation to seize the Hadithah Dam and prevent it from being destroyed by Iraqi soldiers. If the Iraqis would have destroyed the dam, the Euphrates River, which leads south toward Baghdad, would have flooded. Such flooding could have hindered or trapped numerous coalition forces. *DoD*

Below: A pair of "Little Birds" from the 160th Special Operations Aviation Regiment (Airborne) takes off into the night. Since the majority of the regiment's missions occur in the darkness, the operators in this regiment have earned the nickname "night stalkers." Those in the special operations community herald the pilots of the 160th SOAR as the best combat helicopter pilots in the world. *DoD*

Army. Such actions would have caused flooding of the Euphrates River, which leads south toward Baghdad. The flooding of Karbala was an even more immediate threat, and would have almost certainly hindered or trapped numerous coalition forces.

Delta teams were given the mission to locate one hundred high-value targets, with orders to capture or kill. These included Saddam Hussein and his sons Uday and Qusay, as well as high-ranking members of the Baath Party. Teams were inserted by various means after conducting on-site reconnaissance for weeks prior to the actual incursion into Iraq.

During a briefing at the Pentagon, General Richard Meyers, chairman of the Joint Chiefs of Staff, commented on why no Scuds had been successfully launched against coalition partners Jordan and Israel, despite continuous threats: "(This was) because we went in very early, even before the ground war, to secure those places." He would not elaborate, but the underlying reason was that SOF units had already been operating in the northwestern region of Iraq for some time.

An integral part of the special ops effort was the AFSOC Special Tactics Squadron. Members were embedded into various SOF units, fighting alongside

Navy SEALs and British Royal Marines assaulted and seized Iraq's two major gas and oil terminals in the northern Persian Gulf: Kaabot and Mabot. The combined force assaulted the facilities via helicopters and captured the oil facilities on the tip of the Faw Peninsula. Here, a member of the SEAL team provides cover during the operation. *DoD*

the units while providing close air support and air traffic control. For example, when an Army AH-64 Apache helicopter was shot down during the early stage of the war, an AFSOC team later bombed the downed aircraft so the Iraqis could not seize the helicopter and its ordnance. Afterward, the team sanitized the crash site, zeroing all instruments, removing sensitive items, and assuring the destruction of sensitive, irremovable items with thermite grenades.

Regarding the missions of combat controllers, Secretary of the Air Force James G. Roche commented on their capabilities while addressing graduates at Pope Air Force Base, North Carolina, in December 2002:

You [combat controllers] deliver on two important objectives. You guarantee, when called, that we can kill the enemy and destroy his targets with speed, precision and certainty. And in doing so, you ensure that the U.S. Air Force remains the world's best air and space force, a force on which our nation can rely to defend our freedoms and national values, at home or abroad.

Navy SEALs and Royal Marines were charged with locating Iraqi minelayers. Here, a member of the Navy EOD (explosive ordnance disposal) team inspects one of the mines on the Iraqi ship. *UK MOD*

Indispensable combatants in the global war on terrorism are the pararescue jumpers and combat controllers of the Air Force Special Operations Command. They provide immediate trauma care and provide close air support to U.S. and coalition forces. Inserted with other SOF units, theses highly trained operators are an integral part of SOF operations. Here, an AFSOC combat controller gets in some practice time on the range as he runs though some immediate action drills. *DoD*

Below: Two team members from the 3rd Special Forces Group (Airborne) prepare to assault a building in an Advance MOUT exercise. These soldiers are armed with the M4A1 carbine and "tricked out" with an assortment of SOPMOD accessories for the mission at hand. *US Army*

PM 1st Class Andy McKaskle Members of SEAL Team Two conduct SEAL delivery vehicle (SDV) training in the warm waters of the Caribbean. The SDV provides the SEALs with a stealth method of insertion into enemy harbors or other waterborne infiltration. *USN*

SRA Neil Lynch Staff Sergeant Richard Driggers, a combat controller assigned to the 23rd Special Tactics Squadron, Hurlburt Field, Florida, hones his air traffic controller skills on the air traffic control (ATC) simulator. The simulator is one of the three owned by Air Force Special Operations Command, the only ATC simulators in the air force outside of the technical training school environment. *USAF*

To the south, Navy SEALs using high-speed Mark V special warfare craft assaulted two Iraqi offshore oil platforms, Mina al Bakar and Khawr al Amaya in the Persian Gulf. As the waterborne commandos assaulted the platforms, snipers provided cover fire from orbiting helicopters. The seizure of these oil platforms assured that Saddam's forces could not repeat the ecological assault of the first Gulf War; when they dumped raw crude oil into the Persian Gulf. The SEALs were also instrumental in clearing mines from waterways that would have impeded naval and humanitarian vessels.

Author's Notes

America's special operations forces entered the new millennium better trained and equipped than any other military force in the world. Before the twenty-first century was a year old, they were thrust into a global conflict that would test every technique, tactic, and procedure, as well as the mettle of each member of the command. As they enter into combat, they do so with the technological capabilities and full spectrum of military support of the only true military superpower left on earth. Coupled with their maturity and tenacity to prosecute any mission to completion, America's special ops are the true masters of their trade.

As part of a team, these SOF warriors achieve a higher level of proficiency by drawing on one another's strengths and skills. Each services' special operations units brings something unique to the operations. When they are brought together in concert, they bring an entity equipped to conquer any foe and rise above any adversity to seize victory.

As of this writing, U.S. SOF operators and teams continue to perform a wide range of missions throughout the world. Not since the Vietnam War has the special operations community been so employed and active on such a large scale. As Major General Stanley McChrystal commented at a Pentagon briefing, "It's probably the most effective and the widest use of special operations force in recent history."

From training Northern Alliance fighters in the mountainous regions of Afghanistan, to searching the sprawling city of Baghdad for weapons of mass destruction, to performing special reconnaissance missions off the North Korean coastline and along the Syrian border, to direct action tasks in Yemen or the Philippines—these "quiet professionals" continue to be the tip of the U.S. military's spear. They are the warrior elite of the U.S. Special Operations Command.

Antiterrorism (AT): Defensive measures used to reduce the vulnerability of individuals and property to terrorism.

Clandestine operation: Activities sponsored or conducted by governmental departments or agencies in such a way as to assure secrecy or concealment (it differs from covert operations in that emphasis is placed on concealment of the operation rather than on concealment of identity of sponsor). In Special Operations, an activity may be both covert and clandestine and may focus equally on operational considerations and intelligence-related activities.

Close air support (CAS): Air action against hostile targets which are in close proximity to friendly forces and which require detailed integration of each air mission with the fire and movement of those forces.

Counterproliferation: Activities taken to counter the spread of dangerous military capabilities, allied technologies and/or know-how, especially weapons of mass destruction and ballistic missile delivery systems.

Covert operations: Operations which are so planned and executed as to conceal the identity of or permit plausible denial by the sponsor.

Crisis: An incident or situation involving a threat to the U.S., its territories, citizens, military forces and possessions or vital interests that develops rapidly and creates a condition of such diplomatic, economic, political or military importance that commitment of U.S. military forces and resources is contemplated to achieve national objectives.

Counterterrorism (CT): Offensive measures taken to prevent, deter, and respond to terrorism.

Direct action mission: In special operations, a specified act involving operations of an overt, covert, clandestine of low visibility nature conducted primarily by a sponsoring power's special operations forces in hostile or denied areas.

Exfiltration (Exfil): The removal of personnel or units from areas under enemy control.

Geospatial information: Is the precise location and attributes of natural or constructed features and boundaries, referenced to positions on the Earth. This information conveys the "what" and "where" of an object.

Geospatial intelligence: Is the exploitation and analysis of imagery and geospatial information to describe, assess, and visually depict physical features and geographically referenced activities on the Earth

Humanitarian assistance: Assistance provided b Department of Defense forces, as directed by appropriate authority, in the aftermath of natural of manmade disasters to help reduce conditions that present a serious threat to life and property. Assistance provided by Untied States forces is limited in scope and duration and is designed to supplement efforts of civilian authorities that have primary responsibility for providing such assistance.

Imagery: A photograph or similar representation of any natural or manmade feature or object or activity on the Earth and its precise position at the exact time the representation was acquired. This includes products from space-based national intelligence reconnaissance platforms, and "pictures" produced by satellites, airborne platforms, unmanned aerial vehicles, or other similar means.

Imagery intelligence (IMINT): The technical, geographic, and intelligence information derived through the interpretation of imagery and related materials.

Infiltration (Infil): The movement through or into an area or territory occupied by either friendly or enemy troops or organizations. The movement is made either by small groups or by individuals at extended or irregular intervals. When used in connection with the enemy it infers that contact is avoided.

Insurgency: An organized movement aimed at the overthrow of a constituted government through the use of subversion and armed conflict.

Internal defense: The full range of measure taken by a government to free and protect its society from subversion, lawlessness and insurgency.

Inter-operability: The ability of systems, units or forces to provide services to and to and accept services from other systems, units or forces and or use the services so exchanged to enable them to operate effectively together.

Lasing: The act of projecting a laser bean onto a target, for laser guide munitions, or smart bombs. It is also referred to as "painting" a target.

Low-intensity conflict: Political-military confrontation between contending states or groups below conventional war and above routine, peaceful competition among states. It frequently involves protracted struggles of competing principles and ideologies. Low-intensity conflict ranges from subversion to the use of armed force. It is waged by a combination of means employing political, economic, informational and military instruments. Low-intensity conflicts are often localized, generally in the Third World, but contain regional and global security implications.

"The Mog": A term coined by U.S. troops for Mogadishu, Somalia, during Operation Restore Hope, 1993.

NCA: National Command Authorities. The president and the secretary of defense together or their duly deputized alternates or successors. The term signifies constitutional authority to direct the Armed Forces in their execution of military action.

Objectives: Specific actions to be achieved in a specified time period. Accomplishment will indicate progress toward achieving the goals.

Operator: See "Shooter."

Psychological operations: Planned operations to convey selected information and indicators to foreign audiences to influence their emotions, motives, objective reasoning and ultimately the behavior of foreign government, organizations, groups and individuals. The purpose of psychological operations is to induce or reinforce foreign attitudes and behavior favorable to the originator's objectives.

Radar interferometry: Two radar images are taken from slightly different locations. Differences between these images allow for the calculation of surface elevation, or change.

Shooter: Special operations forces trooper (e.g., Delta Operator, U.S. Army Special Forces, U.S. Navy SEAL, U.S. Army Ranger, Force Recon, SAS)

Special reconnaissance: Reconnaissance and surveillance actions conducted by special operations forces to obtain or verify, by visual observation or other collection methods, information concerning the capabilities, intentions and activities of an actual or potential enemy or to secure data concerning the meteorological, hydrographic or geographic characteristics of a particular area. It includes target acquisition, area assessment and post-strike reconnaissance.

STANAG: Standards and Agreements, as set forth by NATO, for the process, procedures, terms, and conditions under which Mutual Government Quality Assurance of defense products are to be performed by the appropriate National Authority of one NATO member nation, at the request of another NATO member nation or NATO Organization.

Strategy: Methods, approaches, or specific moves taken to inclement and attain an objective.

Synthetic aperture radar: (SAR) A technique for obtaining high resolution radar images from a relatively small antenna.

ACE: Air combat element
ANGLICO: Air and naval gunfire liason company
AFSOC: Air Force Special Operations Command
ARSOC: Army Special Operations Command
AOR: Area of responsibility
AT: Antiterrorism
BDA: Bomb damage assessment
CAS: Close air support
CCT: Combat control team
COMINT: Communications intelligence
CRRC: Combat rubber raiding craft
CSAR: Combat search and rescue
CT: Counterterrorism
CQB: Close quarters battle
CRE: Close range engagement
DA: Direct action
DAP: Direct action penetrator
DIA: Defense Intelligence Agency
DOD: Department of Defense
E&E: Evasion and escape
ELINT: Electronic intelligence
FOB: Forward operation base
FRIES: Fast rope insertion/extraction system
GPS: Global positioning system
HAHO: High altitude high opening
HALO: High altitude low opening
HDS: Holographic display sight
HE: High explosive
HEDP: High explosive dual purpose
HET: Human intelligence exploitation team
HTI: Hard target interdiction
HUMINT: Human intelligence
IR: Infrared
JCS: Joint Chiefs of Staff
JSOC: Joint Special Operations Command
JSOF: Joint Special Operations Forces
JSOTF: Joint Special Operations Task Force
KIA: Killed in action
LBE: Load bearing equipment
MICH: Modular/integrated communications helmet
MOUT: Military operations on urbanized terrain
MSS: Mission support site
NATO: North Atlantic Treaty Organization
NAVSPECWAR: Naval Special Warfare Detachment
NBC: Nuclear-biological-chemical

NCA: National Command Authority
NOD: Night optical device
NVG: Night vision goggles
ODA: Operational Detachment–Alpha
PJ: Pararescue jumper
PSYWAR: Psychological warfare
RIS: Rail interface system
RPM: Rounds per minute
RRT: Radio reconnaissance team
RSOV: Ranger special operations vehicle
SAD: Special Activities Staff (U.S.–CIA)
SALT: Supporting arms liaison team
SAR: Search and rescue
SAS: Special Air Service (U.K. or Australian)
SBS: Special Boat Squadron (U.K.)
SEAL: Sea Air Land (U.S. Navy Special Operations Forces)
SF: Special Forces (U.S. Army)
SIGINT: Signals intelligence
SOCOM: Special Operations Command
SOF: Special Operations Forces
SOFLAM: Special operations forces–laser acquisition marker
SOAR(A): Special Operations Aviation Regiment (Airborne)
SOG: Special Operations Group
SR: Special reconnaissance
STANAG: Standards and agreements (as set forth by NATO)
TFR: Task Force Ranger
USASOC: U.S. Army Special Operations Command
USASFC: U.S. Army Special Forces Command
VFR: Visual flight rule
WMD: Weapons of mass destruction

INDEX

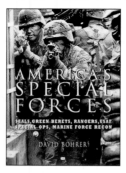

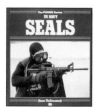

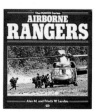